Balrothery Poor Law Union, 1839–1851

Maynooth Studies in Local History

SERIES EDITOR Raymond Gillespie

This is one of six short books published in the Maynooth Studies in Local History series in 2005. Like their predecessors they are, in the main, drawn from theses presented for the MA course in local history at NUI Maynooth. Also, like their predecessors, they range widely over the local experience in the Irish past. That local experience is presented in the context of the complex social and political world of which it is part, from the great houses of Armagh to the rural housing of Leitrim and from the property developers of eighteenth-century Dublin to those who rioted on the streets of the capital. The local experience cannot be a simple chronicling of events relating to an area within administrative or geographically-determined boundaries since understanding the local world presents much more complex challenges for the historian. It is an investigation of the socially diverse worlds of poor and rich. It explores the lives of those who joined the British army in the First World War as well as those who, on principle, chose not to do so. Reconstructing such diverse local worlds relies on understanding what the people of the different communities that made up the localities of Ireland had in common and what drove them apart. Understanding the assumptions, often unspoken, around which these local societies operated is the key to recreating the world of the Irish past and gaining insight into how the people who inhabited those worlds lived their daily lives. As such, studies such as those presented in these short books, together with their predecessors, are at the forefront of Irish historical research and represent some of the most innovative and exciting work being undertaken in Irish history today. They also provide models that others can follow and adapt in their own studies of the Irish past. In such ways can we better understand the regional diversity of Ireland and the social and cultural basis of that diversity. If these books also convey something of the vibrancy and excitement of the world of Irish local history today they will have achieved at least some of their purpose.

Maynooth Studies in Local History: Number 59

Balrothery Poor Law Union, County Dublin, 1839–1851

Sinéad Collins

FOUR COURTS PRESS

Set in 10pt on 12pt Bembo by
Carrigboy Typesetting Services, County Cork for
FOUR COURTS PRESS LTD
7 Malpas Street, Dublin 8, Ireland
e-mail: info@four-courts-press.ie
http://www.four-courts-press.ie
and in North America for
FOUR COURTS PRESS
c/o ISBS, 920 N.E. 58th Avenue, Suite 300, Portland, OR 97213.

ISBN 1-85182-893-1

Printed in Ireland by
ßetaprint Ltd, Dublin

Contents

Acknowledgments

I would like to express my sincere thanks to all who helped me in the course of this study. First to the course directors, Prof. Raymond Gillespie in year one and Dr Terence Dooley in year two, and to my supervisor Professor Colm Lennon for his encouragement and valuable guidance. My gratitude is due in large measure to Paul Harris, County Librarian, Fingal County Council, Jim Walsh of Balbriggan library, the staff of the local studies section of Malahide and Blanchardstown libraries for their assistance in the course of my research. I also wish to acknowledge the help given by Bernadette Marks of the Swords Heritage Centre and by Peadar Bates. Thanks are also due to the staff of the National Library, National Archives and the Gilbert Library who were at all times helpful during my many visits. Last but by no means least, my grateful thanks to Mary Collins whose expertise was generously put at my disposal in all my computer-related difficulties.

Introduction

The population of Ireland in 1720 was estimated to have been about three million but by 1820 it had more than doubled to six and a half million. The population continued to rise between 1821 and 1841 when the census recorded a population of 8,175,124. Poverty was widespread. In the towns, where employment was virtually non-existent, the only resource of the poor was begging. In the country the answer was land. The Irish labourer and small tenant farmer relied on growing enough potatoes to feed their families and leave a small surplus to be sold. There was no legal provision for the poor, the aged and infirm; they could only rely on charity.[1] It was estimated that in the 1830s approximately one shilling per acre per year was given by the farming class to beggars, amounting to between £700,000 and £800,000 per annum.[2]

The question of relief for the poor in Ireland was the subject of a number of official enquiries between 1804 and 1830, none of which resulted in any practical measures to tackle poverty. Pressure mounted both in Ireland and in England to address the situation. In England, the large numbers of destitute Irish settling there gave rise to fears they would become a burden on its relief system and led to demands for the introduction of poor laws to Ireland. In September 1833 a royal commission presided over by Dr Whately, Protestant archbishop of Dublin, was appointed to inquire into the condition of the Irish poor and to suggest remedial measures.

While the Famine in other parts of Ireland has been well documented, particularly in recent years, little has been published concerning north Co. Dublin. It was then a rural, agricultural area, with a population of some 28,000. Only four towns had more than 2,000 inhabitants – Balbriggan had 3,000, Skerries and Swords had 2,500 each and Rush had just over 2,100. Land holdings were predominantly small, 24 per cent did not exceed one acre while a further 25 per cent did not exceed five acres.[3] There was no industry or manufacturing apart from the town of Balbriggan where cotton mills had been established in 1776 and within fifteen years 1,000 people were employed in three spinning factories.[4] The hosiery trade for which Balbriggan became famous was started in 1790. These industries flourished for a time and Balbriggan grew from a small fishing village to a town of 3,000 people. The loss of protective tariffs in the 1820s as a result of the Act of Union and competition from the mechanised mills in Britain led to a decline in the industry. In January 1837 the inquiry by the railway commissioners into the carrying trade of the towns north of Dublin reported that only one of the cotton mills was then at work giving employment in the factory to 90, all but six of whom were female, with a further 250 looms in the town.[5] D'Alton in his *History of County Dublin* says 'Balbriggan has been a very thriving place, but, by the decline of the cotton factories, the withdrawing of the fishery bounties, and the diversion of the great Northern road, the advantages, which its proprietors zealously laboured to promote, have been considerably impeded'.[6] D'Alton tells that in 1829 there were 934 fishermen employed from the port of Balbriggan but following the withdrawal of the government bounty in 1830 there were then only 12 boats there, each employing six or eight men. Thus the only town in the area, that had enjoyed industrial success, was experiencing recession. The decline in the fishing industry also affected the ports of Skerries, Rush and Malahide.

An intensive, commercial tillage zone developed in the latter half of the eighteenth century in the south-eastern part of Ireland, with a narrow strip extending north through Co. Dublin and east Meath as far as Louth.[7] Prosperity increased as European demand peaked in the Napoleonic period. This commercialisation of the tillage economy was accompanied by a dramatic increase in the number of agricultural labourers. It has been estimated that before the Famine at least half of the population in the tillage areas were farm labourers.[8] After the Napoleonic wars the price of agricultural produce fell which induced many farmers to change from tillage to grazing and this led to an over supply of farm labour. An examination of the 1831 census shows that the ratio of agricultural labourers to landholders in Co. Dublin at 4.54/1 was the highest in the country.[9] The national average was 0.86/1.

The findings of the Poor Law Commission provide a vivid picture of the living standards of the poor of north Co. Dublin in the 1830s. This sets the context for the introduction of the poor law in 19th century Ireland and is discussed in the first chapter. The establishment of the Balrothery Poor Law Union, the formation of the administrative machinery to implement the poor law and the building of the workhouse are discussed in chapter two, while the reality of life in the workhouse is examined in the third chapter. Administration, including relations between the Poor Law Commissioners and the Board of Guardians, and the financial status of the union is the subject of the following chapter. The Famine years and their impact on life both in and outside the workhouse are described in the final chapter.

The primary sources are the minute books of the meetings of the Board of Guardians but a number of these are missing for the period under examination. The first book from the inception of the union in May 1839 until February 1843 is retained in the archives of Fingal County Council and the remainder are located in the National Archives. Minutes for the periods 20 February 1843 to 10 August 1844, 23 April 1845 to 17 September 1845, 23 September 1846 to 29 March 1848, 10 July 1850 to 2 April 1851 could not be located. No workhouse registers or other records survive for the Balrothery Union, so that for the periods for which minutes are unavailable, it was necessary to search for other sources. The annual reports of the Poor Law Commissioners and the many parliamentary papers produced during the period afforded much information on the introduction of the poor law and establishment of the union and also statistical detail.

It is hoped in this book to make a contribution to filling the lacuna, which currently exists concerning the lifestyle and conditions of a sector of the population of north Co. Dublin in the 1830s and 1840s. Some historians maintain that a subsistence crisis rather than famine affected the east of Ireland in the late 1840s but Andrew Kettle writing of his life on a farm in Swords in those years says 'we had all the horrors of a terrible famine all through 1847'.[10] Whichever title is used to describe conditions in this area it will be shown that poverty, hunger and severe distress was the lot of many in this district.

1. Life before the introduction of the poor law

The Commission of Enquiry into the state of the poor sat for three years, between 1834 and 1836, and obtained evidence from every part of the country, partly through the medium of a lengthy questionnaire. Some 7,600 copies of this questionnaire were circulated throughout Ireland to clergy of every denomination, magistrates, heads of police and 'to such educated persons as had been named as able and willing to give us assistance'.[1] About 3,100 replies were received and were published as appendices to the Commission's reports. In the area that subsequently was declared the Union of Balrothery replies were received from the parish priests of Swords/ Malahide, Donabate, Lusk/Rush, the rectors of Donabate, Swords and Malahide, from three landlords (George Hamilton of Balbriggan, George Evans of Portrane, and Anthony Hussey of Naul), from two magistrates in Malahide and one in Swords, from a cotton spinner in Balbriggan and from doctors in Swords, Malahide, Rush, Skerries and Balbriggan.

In addition to the questionnaire two assistant commissioners were appointed for each province, one Irish who provided local knowledge and one English who provided agricultural expertise. They were instructed to request persons of each grade in society, of various religious allegiances and of each party in politics to give evidence at an open public meeting in a number of baronies throughout the country. Balrothery was one of the baronies selected for this examination and a public meeting was held in Balbriggan in the summer of 1835 at which 42 named persons gave evidence. This included three magistrates/landlords (Hamilton and Hussey who had replied to the questionnaire and George Woods of Milverton, Skerries), the parish priest of Balrothery, the churchwarden of Lusk, 21 farmers with farms ranging in size from two and a half acres to 350 acres, 13 labourers, a publican and provision dealer, a corn dealer and a cotton manufacturer. In addition 'there were many other small occupiers and labourers who assisted in affirming or correcting the statements and opinions of the principal witnesses'.[2] The assistant commissioners personally inspected the area to satisfy themselves of the accuracy of the statements made. Detailed accounts of these examinations were published as appendices to the Commission's reports.

All respondents to the questionnaire said that there were no deserted children and few illegitimate children in their respective parishes – any orphaned or abandoned children were provided for by the charity of neighbours.[3] Widows were supported by church charity and by the generosity of 'gentlemen in the neighbourhood'. Those incapable of work through old age or infirmity

were generally supported by their children with some help from church charities and resident gentlemen. The practice of church charity is confirmed by the
vestry books of the parish of Swords which show that £20 was levied on that
parish in 1834 and £10 in 1835 for the support of deserted children.[4] In 1837 a
levy of one farthing per acre was imposed on the parishes of Clonmethan,
Ballyboghal, Westpalstown and Palmerstown for the same purpose.[5]

Revd Howard and Magistrate Purcell of Swords replied that there were
about 700 labourers in that parish and two-thirds had constant employment.[6]
The replies from Donabate, Portrane and Naul indicated that most labourers had
constant work. George Hamilton said there were 481 agricultural labourers in
the parish of Balrothery and 500 other labourers engaged in weaving, spinning
and as retail dealers, and almost as many females, but that employment fluctuated. Mr Locke, the cotton spinner from Balbriggan, said many labourers in
the town were out of work in winter and in great distress with no means of
support other than begging. The respondents from Malahide said there were
between 80 and 100 labourers but only about 30 had constant employment.

The parish priest of Rush gave a detailed reply. Of 140 agricultural
labourers, the majority of whom had no land, only 50 had constant employment. The remainder got work for less than four months at harvest and at
planting and digging of potatoes, and tried to supplement their earnings by
casual work such as collecting and selling seaweed. There were 120 fishermen
whose earnings after a week at sea were less than two shillings and they were
often idle because of bad weather. The poverty of the inhabitants of Rush was
described in an application for assistance during the cholera outbreak of 1832
as 'having been much increased by the destruction of the fisheries consequent
on the withdrawal of the bounties formerly paid for taking and curing fish'.[7]

The assistant commissioners in their report said that they could only get
information in relation to employment in six parishes and gave the
following statistics:[8]

Table 1.1 Number of labourers in the barony of Balrothery

Parish	Total number of labourers	Permanently employed	*Occasionally employed	+Almost always unemployed
Balrothery	600	200	350	50
Baldongan	400	100	240	60
Rush	250	100	150	–
Naul	118	73	41	4
Garristown	195	45	140	10
Balscadden	220	60	160	–
Total	1783	578	1081	124

*The assistant commissioners estimated this as six to seven months work in the year.
+Either constantly idle from want of skill, strength or demand or could only get work for
a very short time in harvest and at digging and setting of potatoes.

From these figures it appears that only one third of the labourers in these six parishes had constant work. Those with only occasional employment supported themselves by potatoes grown in their gardens or on conacre, which was land hired for a season to grow a single crop. The quantity of conacre varied from an eighth of an acre to half an acre, depending on family size. Conacre was mentioned by almost all of the respondents as vital for survival in times of unemployment. All said employment had declined very much in recent years, perhaps to half, partly due to the increase in population and partly because of the fall in value of agricultural produce, especially grain, since the peace of 1815. Farmers had been forced to reduce costs by changing from tillage to grazing.[9] While five to six men were employed for every 100 acres of tillage only one was required per 100 acres grazing. Most farmers lacked capital and could not employ labourers, their lands consequently being only half cultivated.

The average daily rate, without food, for those in constant employment was as follows:[10]

Table 1.2 Daily wages

Season	Men	Boys under 16	Women
Winter	10*d*.	4*d*.	Varies from 4*d*.
Spring	1*s*.	6*d*.	to 8*d*. per day
Summer	1*s*. to 1*s*.2*d*.	6*d*. to 8*d*.	according to the
Harvest	2*s*.	1*s*.	work.

Women and children were only employed occasionally in weeding, haymaking and picking potatoes and fruit. Women were said to be unable for much outdoor work because of constant bearing and suckling of children on an insufficient diet.[11]

Most holdings were small although there had been a tendency to enlarge farms as leases expired and to demolish houses so that they could not be let to labourers.[12] Many of the labourers were dispossessed tenant farmers. The following figures were given in relation to the number and size of holdings in Lusk, which was the only parish for which precise figures were supplied:[13]

Table 1.3 Number of land holdings in the parish of Lusk

Number of holdings	Parish of Lusk	Percentage of total
Not exceeding 1 acre	47	12
Not exceeding 5 acres	144	35
6 to 9 acres	62	15
10 to 19 acres	56	14
20 to 49 acres	50	12
50 to 79 acres	22	5
80 to 99 acres	7	2
Exceeding 100 acres	19	5

The figures for Lusk were shown to be representative of the entire area by a return published in 1846 which showed that in the union of Balrothery 49 per cent of holdings did not exceed five acres.[14]

The working day was long. Frances Power Cobbe in her life story tells that on her father's estate in Donabate 'in summer men worked from six (or earlier if mowing was to be done) till breakfast and thence til one o'clock. After an hour's dinner the great bell tolled again and the work went on til six. In winter there was no cessation of work from 8 am til 5 pm'.[15]

Food consisted principally of the commonest variety of potatoes, called 'lumpers', with some wheaten bread and oatmeal. The great majority suffered from insufficient food even when in constant employment. This was especially so when potatoes were scarce and dear in the months of July, August and September. The assistant commissioners when visiting cabins at mealtime found in numerous instances that the meal consisted of 'a dish of potatoes only sufficient for the proper nourishment of one or two persons although intended for five or six'.[16] When the scarcity was unusually great the very poor were obliged to resort to boiling weeds, especially the *prassagh* or wild mustard. They noted many instances of families supported by sons and daughters as soon as they were old enough to work and observed that filial affection, duty and mutual assistance were 'considered as religious and moral obligations of the most sacred character'.[17] It was agreed by several present that the poor endured their lot patiently and trusted that 'Providence' would help them. 'They consider that to despair of God's providence is a mortal sin'.[18]

The corn dealer and provision dealer present testified that corn would keep very well for three years and if substituted for potatoes as the principal food of the peasantry would undoubtedly reduce the chance of starvation. However, due to the prevailing rate of wages and the average number of family to be fed, clothed and sheltered, it was far too expensive for the labourer class.[19]

Cottages were built of clay, thatched with straw that was generally in very bad condition, the interior measuring about 16 feet by 12 feet and usually divided into two apartments, a kitchen and bedroom. The floor consisted of the natural earth and was usually low, uneven and damp. Many had only a hole in the roof or at the back of the fireplace to carry off smoke. Some had no windows. Where there were windows they were small and many used straw or old bagging to protect against cold and wet. Some cottages had a pigsty, in others the pig was turned out by day and chained in a corner at night. None had privies, sheds or outhouses. In the worst cabins the whole family slept on the floor. The usual bedding was straw covered with coarse calico. These accounts were confirmed by the personal observation of the assistant commissioners who reported:

Nothing can exceed the wretched condition of the commoner description of labourers' cabins, with little or no light but what is admitted by the door, and no air whatever when the door is shut, but by the chimney. These wretched hovels would not in any other country be considered sufficient to shelter cattle, when filled with eight or ten human beings, with no other furniture about them than a few stools, and a table formed of old boards and sticks, a few pots and kettles, and some straw, and one or two old blankets or coats, in perfect rags for bedding, they present one of the most melancholy spectacles which it is possible to behold.[20]

With the exception of those labourers who had constant work and small families the clothing of the peasantry was described as generally wretched:

A shirt, or part of one, in rags, with trousers, and a waistcoat scarcely hanging together, and the whole covered with a coarse frieze greatcoat, patched and much worn. The women endeavour to keep up a little more decent appearance, but their poverty is generally strongly expressed by their dirty, patched and coarse clothing. The children, unless the family be small, and the men well-employed, are more than half naked, barefooted, their few clothes hanging about them in tatters. The use of shoes and stockings is increasing a little. The women can seldom make their own clothes, which is attributed to the constant employment and fatigue of the mother in suckling and attending to so many young children which prevents her from having time to learn to work at her needle.[21]

When asked how the labourer spent his time when unemployed the reply was: 'just doing nothing at all: we are ashamed to be seen idling, or known to be without work or food and lie down at the back of a ditch to hide ourselves'.[22] The pride of the poor was confirmed by one of the large farmers who gave the example of a woman who, although in deep distress and receiving charity privately, used display a teapot containing only hot water inside the door of her cabin so that passers-by might think she had tea.[23]

The commissioners presented their report in 1836. They found that in all parts of Ireland there was much and deep-seated distress. Part of the problem was the over-supply of agricultural labour. In Great Britain agricultural families constituted one quarter of the population while in Ireland they represented about two-thirds. In Ireland there were about five agricultural labourers for every two for the same quantity of land in Great Britain. They considered it would be impossible for the able-bodied in general to provide against sickness, unemployment and old age or make provision for their widows and children in the event of their premature death.[24]

The Commission did not recommend a workhouse system as had been introduced in England and Wales in 1834. They were of the opinion that because of the extent of destitution in Ireland the workhouse system that had been designed to make the idle seek work would be unsuitable in Ireland. 'The difficulty in Ireland is not to make the able-bodied look for employment, but to find it profitably for the many who seek it'.[25] They recommended that Ireland be divided into relief districts and that a tax be levied to provide a system of support for the destitute, the sick, the infirm and others incapable of supporting themselves. They recommended that a board of improvement be appointed to effect a comprehensive system of national improvement by public works, development of trade, manufacturing, fisheries and mining, government assistance for emigration and encouragement of agricultural education. They felt much of the land of Ireland yielded only one third of what it could produce under proper management. The report concluded by saying:

> The improvement of Ireland is of the deepest importance to every part of the United Kingdom; at present, with a population nearly equal to half that of Great Britain, she yields only about a twelfth of the revenue to the State that Great Britain does; nor can she yield more until she has more to yield. Increased means must precede increased contributions; and to supply Ireland with these is the great object of our recommendations. We anxiously hope that Ireland may at length become one of the richest countries in Europe, and a mighty increase both of strength and revenue to the Crown of England.[26]

The government did not accept the recommendations of the Commission which were contrary to the prevailing philosophy of laissez-faire. George Nicholls, an English Poor Law Commissioner, was sent to Ireland to re-examine the situation and present a more palatable report. His brief included an instruction to inquire whether a workhouse system could be established 'which shall not, in point of food, clothing and warmth, give its inmates a superior degree of comfort to the common lot of the independent labourer.'[27] Nicholls arrived in Ireland in September 1836 and after a tour of the country lasting six weeks produced a report. He recommended that a tax be levied on land and property and that each area be provided with a workhouse, which was to be the only source of relief. He made no recommendations to develop the resources of the country. A bill based on his recommendations became law on 31 July 1838 under the title 'An Act for the more effectual Relief of the Destitute Poor in Ireland'. One of the things uniting the disparate forces in favour of the bill, from the liberal whigs to the humanist tories, was the belief that Irish landlords were failing in their responsibilities to their tenants and to society in general and there was a determination that Irish property must support Irish poverty.[28] This act marked an important milestone in the evolution of Irish social policy and became the country's first statutory social service.

2. Establishment of the union and building of the workhouse

The government decided that the act should be implemented by the Poor Law Commissioners for England and Wales and George Nicholls was appointed resident commissioner in Ireland. He arrived in Dublin on 4 September 1838 with four assistants, all experienced English poor law officials.[1] He assigned a district to each to examine with a view to the establishment of the unions, as the administrative areas were to be known. They were instructed that unions were to be as compact as possible with a radius of approximately ten miles and a market town at the centre where the workhouse would be built.[2] Assistant Commissioner Earle was given responsibility for the Dublin region and a Dr Phelan, a medical doctor from Clonmel, was shortly afterwards appointed to assist him. The assistant commissioners, having visited their respective areas, reported to Mr Nicholls on 9 October 1838:

> In their earlier investigations they found that extremely vague and exaggerated notions were entertained of the law itself and its probable effects. All appeared to view the approach of the commissioners with more or less alarm, and to regard the introduction of the new law as a new evil. By unwearied exertion, and great patience and perseverance in explaining the objects and intentions of the new law they succeeded in removing much of the alarm and misapprehension which at first prevailed and all opposition has now subsided.[3]

Concerns about the extent and boundaries of the proposed union led to the convening of a meeting in Balbriggan in December 1838. Lengthy accounts appeared in the press and the following gentlemen were named as attending: the Revd Edward Taylor, James Hans Hamilton, George Hamilton, Thomas Hamilton, A.S. Hussey, John Mee, Taylor Gilbert, William O'Reilly, Henry Walsh, Peter Seaver, John Mangan, Richard Rooney, John King, Thomas Butler, Richard Smith, John Duffy, James King, J. Mathews, William Magrath, Mason Yates, Peter Arnold, Richard Jenner, T. Mathews, Drs O'Reilly, Franklin, and Thornhill, Revds Smith (P.P. Rush), Canavan (P.P. of Nane and Damastown) (sic), John Molloy, and John Gough. The meeting was also attended by 'a large number of farmers, millers, townspeople and peasantry'.[4] James Hans Hamilton presided and said the object of the meeting was:

With a view of being prepared when the poor law commissioners, who are now travelling through the country, come to our neighbourhood, to give them every necessary information they may require previous to establishing a workhouse in this union and also to check them in case they evince a disposition to do anything injurious to us or that they may lean too heavily on the proprietors or their tenants.

George Hamilton addressed the meeting and said he was one of those who had been opposed to many of the provisions of the bill but now that it was law they must make it 'as salutary as possible'. Poor relief was intended to benefit 'our poor suffering fellow-creatures' but must be administered by those who were on the one hand acquainted with local needs but who were also anxious to prevent extravagance. Unlimited discretion had been given to the commissioners to decide the extent and boundaries of unions and he warned of the danger of a body in the metropolis being allowed to make decisions without knowledge of local conditions. Population rather than area should be the criterion. In England and Wales there were 584 workhouses for a population of 11,687,000 or about 20,000 in each union while in Ireland the commissioners proposed to have 100 workhouses for a population of over 8,000,000. He considered the population and area of the northern part of Co. Dublin and part of Co. Meath justified a workhouse without being attached either to Drogheda or Dublin. He feared if 'this union be appended to Dublin we will be taxed not only for the support of our own poor but also for the poor of Dublin'.

The parish priest of Rush spoke of the appalling degree of destitution witnessed by clergymen and physicians and of the dreadful situation of people no longer able to work, saying 'it is the custom when a man becomes unable to work to cast him off'. He felt the new law would be the salvation of the poor, 'when unable to work their country will provide for them, though they may not get luxuries in the workhouse they will get fuel, clothing and diet'. A resolution was passed that a committee of proprietors, occupying tenants of rateable property and the clergymen present be formed for the purpose of conferring with the commissioners concerning the extent and boundaries of the union, the number of electoral districts and the basis proposed for the valuation of property.

A further meeting of landowners and occupiers was held in Swords on 6 March 1839 presided over by Lord Talbot de Malahide. The assistant commissioners, Earle and Phelan, attended. They described their proposals for the union, the electoral divisions and the rating system and agreed to consider any further suggestions those present might make. At the end of the meeting a vote of thanks to Mr Earle for 'his laborious, able and very satisfactory statement' was passed with applause.[5]

The representations made bore fruit. On 1 April 1839 an order was made forming the Union of Balrothery from the area of Co. Dublin extending from the Meath border to Swords and Malahide with the exception of the parishes of Garristown and Ballymadun which were included in the Union of Dunshaughlin.[6] The instruction to select a market town for the location of the workhouse was ignored. The five-acre site chosen was in a rural area some five miles south of Balbriggan and mid-way between Balbriggan and Swords. At a meeting held in Dublin city the following month Mr. Earle said a union had been formed at the north end of the county because 'it was seen that there were more beggars in the north than could conveniently be attached to Dublin'.[7]

The Union of Balrothery consisted of the following twelve electoral districts:

Table 2.1 Electoral districts

Parish	Electoral district	Number of guardians	Area statute acres	Population Census 1831
Balrothery	Balbriggan	3	6884	5078
Balscadden	Balscadden	1	3948	1011
Holmpatrick and Baldongan together with the townlands of Ballyhavil, Lane, Collinstown in the parish of Lusk	Holmpatrick	2	7123	4046
Lusk excluding townlands included in Holmpatrick	Lusk	3	12049	4820
Westpalstown, Ballyboghal	Ballyboghal	1	4824	1052
Naul, Hollywood, Grallagh	Hollywood	2	7417	2016
Palmerstown, Clonmethan	Clonmethan	1	4169	890
Swords	Swords	3	9668	3617
Killossery, Kilsallaghan	Kilsallaghan	2	7249	1585
Donabate, Portrane	Donabate	2	4304	1020
Kinsealy, Cloghran/Swords	Kinsealy	1	3693	1191
Malahide, Portmarnock	Malahide	2	3805	1798
Total		23	75133	28124

Division into electoral districts was of great significance as each electoral district was responsible for bearing the cost of its own poor in the workhouse. There are many instances in the minutes of guardians changing the chargeability of inmates from one district to another.

Boards were composed of ex-officio and elected guardians in the ratio of one to three, the former being selected by local magistrates from among their number, the latter elected by persons paying county cess. Votes were

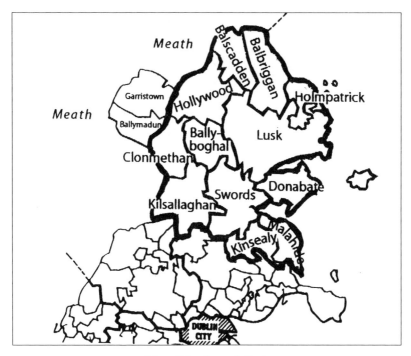

1 Map of the electoral districts

allowed on a sliding scale, ranging from those paying up to £1 who had one vote, to those paying £10 and over who had six votes.[8] Mr Nicholls observed 'the cumulative votes of the owners and larger occupiers would serve to counterbalance the number of small ratepayers, and secure the return of competent individuals'.[9] From 1843 the voting qualifications were based on the valuation of property, still on a sliding scale varying from occupiers valued up to £20 with one vote, to those valued at £200 and over with six votes.[10] All males of full age and paying county cess of ten shillings or more were eligible to stand for election, apart from clergy and stipendiary magistrates. Clergy were excluded 'not from any notion of the general unfitness of the clergy to fill the office of guardian; but with reference solely to the present state of religious opinion in Ireland, and to the importance of keeping the functions of the boards of guardians totally free from even the suspicion of any kind of bias'.[11]

The first election for ex-officio guardians took place at a meeting of magistrates on 8 April 1839 in the courthouse at Swords.[12] The following were selected: Charles Cobbe of Newbridge House, Donabate, George Hamilton of Hampton Hall, Balbriggan, Andrew S. Ball, Malahide Castle, John W. Stubbs, Swords, Thomas Baker, Balbriggan, Anthony S. Hussey, The Naul and George Woods of Milverton, Skerries.[13]

The election for the other guardians took place on 8 May 1839 and the following were returned:[14]

Balbriggan	William O'Reilly, Sea Farm, Balbriggan.
	Thos C. Hamilton, Hampton Hall.
	John Travers Madden, Inch House.
Balscadden	Thomas Dillon, Bridgefoot, Balbriggan.
Holmpatrick	John Johnston, Hacketstown.
	James Lynch, Loughshinny.
Lusk	Patrick Dodd, Tommintown, Swords.
	Walter Rickard, Haystown.
	John Rooney, Raheny.
Ballyboghal	Thos Byrne, Ballyboghal.
Hollywood	Francis Hynes, Hollywood.
	Bartholomew Ennis, Killougher.
Clonmethan	Thos Butler, Jordanstown, Ashbourne.
Swords	Elias T. Corbally, Rathbeale.
	James Brangan, Swords.
	Hugh Moran, Fosterstown.
Kilsallaghan	Patrick Corbally, Rathbeale.
	John Segrave, Barn, Ashbourne.
Donabate	Mungo Duckett, New Lawn, Swords.
	Thomas Martin – address not given.
Kinsealy	Thomas McOwen, Middleton, Artaine.
Malahide	M. O'Grady M.D., La Mancha.
	Charles Fraser, Broomfield.

The practice of landlords being involved in selection of candidates appears to have prevailed. An election took place in only two of the 12 electoral districts and 17 of the 23 seats were uncontested.[15] Both Elias Corbally and William O'Reilly, elected as ordinary members, were magistrates.[16] Both were Catholics and this may have had a bearing on their non-selection as ex-officio guardians. The practice of magistrates standing for election was not unusual. By 1843 a total of 266 magistrates had been elected as ordinary members to 89 of the 130 boards of guardians, including three in Balrothery.[17]

Who were the men who became the first guardians of the Balrothery Union? An examination of Griffith's Valuation shows that six of the seven ex-officio guardians had extensive land holdings. The other ex-officio, Andrew Ball, was agent for Lord Talbot de Malahide. Of the 23 elected guardians all but two occupied farms varying in size from 450 acres to 28 acres, the majority having farms in excess of 100 acres.

In 1840 the members of the first board were returned with two exceptions – Martin and Fraser. A newspaper account said that 'a contest was threatened in only one district but that it was probable that the good sense of the parties put forward would prevail to save the expense and distraction of a contest'.[18] It went on to say 'the meeting for nominations was not well attended, there being only seven or eight of the late guardians and half as many ratepayers present'. George Hamilton, who was conservative in politics and a member of the Church of Ireland, spoke and referred to the 'good feeling and praise-worthy spirit that prevailed in the late board and the entire absence of religious or party feeling'. William O'Reilly spoke also of the good relations in the boardroom where, he said, the majority were Liberal and Catholic. He added 'as the Conservative party had not attempted to disturb the former nominations his friends would not interrupt the good feeling which so happily existed'. Only one district was contested that year when three candidates stood for the two seats in Holmpatrick. The previous guardians, Johnston and Lynch, were re-elected.[19] The board decided to pay only £10 expenses to the returning officer 'as only one electoral district had been contested'.[20] They refused to pay the police for the duties they performed during the election 'they being already the well-paid servants of the public'.

The harmony between the parties in Balrothery continued for some years as again in 1842 only one electoral district was contested.[21] In 1846 George Hamilton, then chairman, in the course of evidence to a select committee of the House of Lords said that although the majority of the guardians were farmers and differed from him in politics and religion they had three times elected him chairman. He added 'I have seldom been able to trace the operation of political or religious feelings in their conduct at the board'.[22] He paid tribute to the ability of the elected guardians and the attention they paid to the management of the workhouse.

This agreement in the Balrothery union contrasts with controversies in the city of Dublin where what was called the 'Orange organisation' was reported prior to the 1839 elections to be 'in unprecedented activity in the hope to secure the election of the brethren to the Dublin unions'.[23] The ex-officio guardians nominated there were described as 'almost exclusively the orange and rotten corporation clique'.[24] In a study of elections held between 1839 and 1843 Gerard O'Brien says the number of seats contested demonstrated a striking difference between rural and urban districts. In large urban areas, such as Dublin and Cork, seats were invariably contested whereas in outlying divisions seats tended to pass uncontested to the same candidates each year.[25]

The first meeting of the board took place at Session House, Swords, on 28 May 1839 when 29 of the guardians and the assistant commissioner, Phelan, were present. Elias Corbally and Charles Cobbe were proposed as chairman. Corbally was elected by sixteen votes to nine and held this post for the next three years. The board met twice monthly until 1 February 1841 when the workhouse was almost ready to open and weekly thereafter. One of the first tasks of the guardians was to appoint a clerk and following an advertisement, which appeared in the *Dublin Evening Post* on 22 June 1839 two replies were received and James Kennelly was appointed on 1 July 1839.

The commissioners were responsible for selecting sites for workhouses and providing and furnishing suitable buildings. The only input of the guardians into the building of the workhouses was to provide the finance. George Wilkinson, an architect with experience of the English workhouses, was engaged at a salary of £500 per annum to prepare plans, specifications, contract documents and to supervise the building of all 130 Irish work-houses. His brief included the instruction that the style of building was to be of the cheapest description compatible with durability and 'all mere decoration being studiously excluded'.[26]

In August 1839 the commissioners approved plans for a workhouse for Balrothery Union that was designed to accommodate 600 but they con-sidered it expedient that space for only 400 be provided initially.[27] The cost of obtaining possession of the five-acre site, erecting and fitting out the workhouse and providing 'utensils and machinery for setting the poor to work therein' was estimated to be £5,900. The guardians were directed to raise this as a poor rate or to borrow it and charge it and the interest on the future poor rate.[28] The site was rented from Lord Howth at £15.15s.0d. per annum and £50 compensation was paid to the occupier.[29] The contract was awarded to a Mr Doolin in the sum of £4,945. Building started in November 1839 when the commissioners appointed a clerk-of-works, Benjamin Brown, at a salary of two guineas per week.[30] The commissioners made it clear that while the guardians must pay the clerk of works, he was under the direction of their architect, to whom any suggestions he might receive from the guardians would be conveyed.

While the workhouse was under construction preparations for opening had to be made by the board. The first major task was to have the union valued. Having published a number of advertisements for 'competent persons' the tender of Messrs Taylor and Morris, professional valuers, was accepted in October 1839. Three local committees of guardians were appointed to super-intend progress and provide local information. A valuation in the sum of £131,000 was received in April 1840 and was referred to these committees for examination, following which a special meeting was held on 13 July 1840 to consider the entire valuation and achieve uniformity. The district committees reported that meetings had been held in each area and several valuations had been altered on foot of representations made to them. The board adopted a final valuation of £130,760 on 4 August 1840.[31]

The commissioners appointed assessors to examine the valuation and the guardians were accused by these assessors of over-ruling the valuers and 'making revisions without adherence to any fixed rule'. They reported that both landlords and tenantry, ex-officio and elected guardians, appeared to be unanimous concerning the expediency of lowering the valuation. The

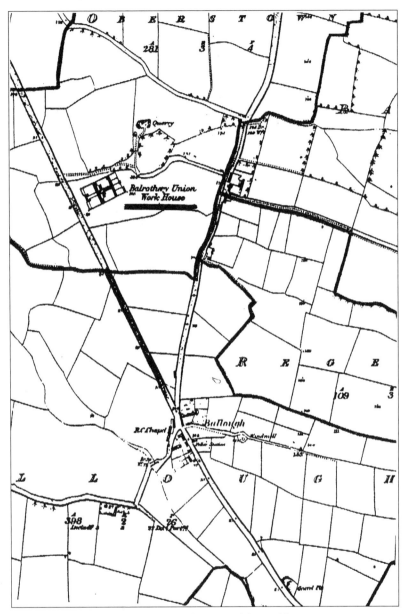

2 Map showing the location of the workhouse

assessors considered the valuation as adopted by the guardians to be much beneath the true letting value.[32] The guardians, however, were subsequently commended by Assistant Commissioner Hall, who was then supervising the union, for giving 'unusual time and consideration' to the valuation. In his report Hall said boards of guardians differed in applying valuation principles and Balrothery was an example of a low valuation. 'While they did reduce considerably valuations they addressed themselves to the task of revision with the utmost assiduity and care'.[33]

The regulations made by the commissioners required that on admission paupers were to be dressed in the workhouse uniform. A committee of five guardians was appointed in September 1840 to have suitable clothing and bedding provided. Samples were supplied by the commissioners and having examined these the committee recommended for females a linen shift, an under petticoat of twilled calico, an outside petticoat of linsey woolsey, a jacket or bedgown of quaker check lined with grey calico, a bodice of ticken lined with calico, knitted stockings of worsted yarn and double threads, a white linen cap and an apron of quaker check. For men a linen shirt, trousers of barragon, a frieze jacket with a short skirt for the infirm, a round jacket for the able-bodied, a worsted cap, knitted stockings of woollen yarn reaching above the knee for the infirm and below the knee for the able-bodied.

The committee displayed a sharp eye to economy. The sample of men's jackets had a second row of buttons which they considered unnecessary and recommended they be omitted. They also thought that shoes should 'be made straight, not right and left, and be shod not nailed'. They considered women's gowns unnecessary, 'other articles of dress being sufficient'. The committee also recommended that as soon as possible the inmates should make the clothing and that items which could not be made in the workhouse should be made within the union, where possible. As clothing would remain the property of the union, to be worn only while in the workhouse and surrendered on leaving, they felt the quality and durability of material to be of great importance.

Following advertisement in the newspapers tenders were accepted on 30 November 1840 from various contractors for a range of clothing including 50 men's jackets at 7s. 11d. each, 50 trousers at 3s. 10d., 100 men's shirts at 2s. 5d., 100 women's petticoats at 2s. 9½d., 100 women's shifts at 1s. 10d., 100 girls shifts at 10d., 50 aprons at 11d., 50 men's caps at 4½d., 50 pairs of men's shoes at 5s. 6d. per pair and 50 pairs of women's shoes at 3s. 9d. per pair. At the same time 100 sets of bed clothing consisting of blankets, coverlets, sheets, bed ticks and bolsters were ordered. The board resolved that every article should be of Irish manufacture. A meeting had been held in Balbriggan a few days previously with the object of encouraging the revival of the Irish manufacturing trade. George Hamilton presided at the meeting and said one of the reasons for the movement to revive trade was the 'imminent pressure of an expensive system of poor laws just come into operation' and it was in the interest of all to endeavour to provide profitable employment for the poor and avoid the necessity for them to resort to the workhouse.[34]

In November 1840 Patrick Durnin was appointed master at a salary of £45 per annum, Mrs Archbold matron with a salary of £30, Thomas Lenehan porter at a salary of £18 and a suit of clothes. Each was to get a reasonable portion of the house provisions. Dr Adrian of Oldtown was appointed medical attendant at a salary of £50.

Diet was an important matter to be decided. The guiding principle enshrined in the regulations was that the diet of a pauper should be such as would maintain him in health but should not exceed in quality or quantity the ordinary diet of the labouring population in the district and that two meals per day were adequate for adults.[35] The board approved the following diet on 8 March 1841:

	Breakfast	Dinner	Supper
Adults+ from 14 years	7 ounces meal	3 pounds potatoes 1 pint buttermilk	–
Boys and girls 7–13 years	3 ounces meal	2 pounds potatoes 1 pint buttermilk	4 ounces bread
Children under 7 years	meal*	potatoes*	bread*

*Amount to be at discretion of the master.
+Infirm adults and women not doing hard labour were to receive one ounce oatmeal and eight ounces of potatoes less than able-bodied adults.

Early in February 1841 the commissioners declared the workhouse fit for the reception of the destitute poor.[36] The master was authorised to purchase supplies of household items from a Mr Daniel of Mary Street including candles, one ton of straw, one hundredweight each of soap and salt, and a supply of sulphur for fumigating the clothing of the entrants. Foodstuffs were ordered from local suppliers including one ton of oatmeal from William Arnold, one ton of cup potatoes from Peter Arnold, bread from Laurence Sweetman of Ballyboghal and buttermilk from John Rooney.

The first paupers were admitted on 8 March 1841 but were released when it was found that no shirts or shifts were available and clothing had not been branded. One week later on 15 March 1841 they were re-admitted – 17 adult males, 6 adult females, 1 girl under 15 years and 1 child under 2 years. The workhouse was in business.

BUILDING OF THE WORKHOUSE

The cost of building and fitting out the workhouse had been estimated by the commissioners at £5,900 but the final cost amounted to £6,975. Defects became evident within a month of opening. At the meeting of 12 April 1841 a

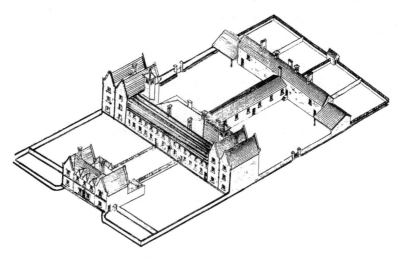

3 Bird's eye view of a workhouse

long list of faults was reported including leaks in the roof and window sashes, a faulty stove in the girls room making it uninhabitable due to smoke, broken steps, defective ventilation and inadequate facilities in the laundry. It was decided to bring these matters to the attention of the commissioners and this was the start of a long-running battle between the guardians and the commissioners. Six weeks later the board were advised of the defective state of the pump and of the floors of the house. In mid-June there was still a problem with the pump that the contractor was either unwilling or unable to repair. A week later the well was reported to be dry. In December 1841 the lower part of the house was flooded which led the guardians to pass a resolution regretting that 'the representations made to the commissioners regarding the site of the workhouse before it was commenced were ignored, the guardians being aware that the house would be liable to overflow of water in winter if built in the present position'. In January 1843 the master was instructed to employ a mason to have the chimneys in the wards raised as they were smoking.

Balrothery was not alone in having problems. Defects and price over-runs emerged in several unions. So many complaints were received that in October 1843 the government appointed James Pennethorne, an English architect, to examine the grievances. On 16 November the clerk of the union wrote to Mr Pennethorne setting out the complaints of the guardians, which included the 'exorbitant rent'.[37]

Mr Pennethorne and his assistant inspected 62 workhouses. In his report he attributed most of the faults to the huge workload of the architect, George Wilkinson, and the mistaken economy of having only one architect to superintend the erection of so many workhouses spread all over Ireland.[38] Pennethorne upheld the complaints of the Balrothery guardians. He said that the site about 300 yards away on higher ground, which had been favoured by the guardians, might have been preferable and better drained but understood the lower site was chosen because of more convenient access and 'more ornamental to the neighbourhood'. He said the land was not of 'peculiarly good quality and the lands around are believed to be let at a much lower rental'. He gave the following description of the work:[39]

> The walls have been built with a hard black stone that is affected by exposure to the atmosphere, and becomes brittle, and mortar composed of bad sand and very little lime. The joints are rough and thick, and not grouted, and the stones are laid very irregularly, with many small ones. The sills are almost all fractured, and many of the worked surfaces are flaking off. The steps and landings of the staircases have been executed with a similar stone and are beginning to crack, and the workmanship of the stairs has been altogether badly executed. The timber generally is of a coarse quality and the workmanship bad. Wet penetrates the roofs from insufficient or improperly laid flashings. The clay floors are cracked and defective.

He attributed the drainage problems to the failure to build the ground floor to a sufficiently high level. In regard to excess cost he found that no provision had been made in the original contract for drains, that the guardians had required a stable to be built for their horses that cost £87 and that the contingencies provision was inadequate. Balrothery was one of nine unions in which he classed the work as below average. He calculated the cost per inmate of building the workhouse as £16 11s. 6d. Only two of the 130 other workhouses built at that time had a higher per capita building cost.

George Nicholls reacted strongly to the report and a select committee of the House of Commons decided that a further inquiry was necessary. George Barney of the Royal Engineers was appointed in September 1844 to inspect each workhouse in Ireland. He reported that considering the circumstances in which the work was carried out the prices paid in general were fair. He concluded that the cost excess for all workhouses was £24,774 or 12½ per cent and a further £21,932 was incurred because of bad workmanship. In Balrothery he reported the total cost as £6,927, and estimated the excess over the proper cost as £200 and that repairs due to defective construction amounted to £227. His report mentioned the Balrothery site, along with Caherciveen, Tralee and Carrick-on-Shannon, as badly located on grounds of distance from a town.[40]

The final outcome of these enquiries was that all unions were relieved of the excess cost by direction of the Treasury on 21 February 1845.[41] The minute book for this period is missing so that the reaction of the guardians must be left to the imagination.

3. Life in the workhouse

The numbers increased gradually – at the end of the first year there were 180 in the workhouse. Residents remained in the region of 200, or only half capacity, during the first half of the decade, with seasonal fluctuations. Between September and March each year the numbers tended to increase and to fall in summer. During these years approximately 35 per cent of the inmates were children while 55 per cent of the adults were male.[1] No registers survive so that a breakdown of the adult figures on age grounds, previous residence, occupation, religion or marital status is not available.

What was life like for those within the walls? The fundamental attitude of the commissioners was set out in their sixth annual report:

> None but the really destitute poor will seek admission, provided that order and discipline be strictly maintained. It is in truth the regularity, order, strict enforcement of cleanliness, constant occupation, preservation of decency and decorum, exclusion of all the irregular habits and tempting excitements of life, on which reliance must mainly be placed for deterring individuals, not actually and unavoidably destitute, from seeking refuge within the workhouse.[2]

The commissioners ensured that such an atmosphere prevailed by means of detailed, mandatory regulations governing every aspect of life in the workhouse and from reading these a very clear picture of the grim existence endured by inmates emerges.[3] Persons seeking admission were first placed in provisional wards located near the entrance gate until a decision to admit them was made by the guardians at their next weekly meeting. On admission they were examined by the doctor, cleansed and dressed in the workhouse garb. Clothes worn on entry were fumigated and stored until such time as the owner left or died, in which case they became the property of the union. It was an offence to leave the workhouse without surrendering the workhouse clothing and any doing so were prosecuted.

Frances Power Cobbe, who was a daughter of one guardian and sister of another, refers in her book to the reluctance of the poor to enter the workhouse:

> There was a fearful ordeal by water in the shape of a warm bath to be undergone on entrance; there were large rooms with glaring windows, admitting a most uncomfortable degree of light, and never shaded by

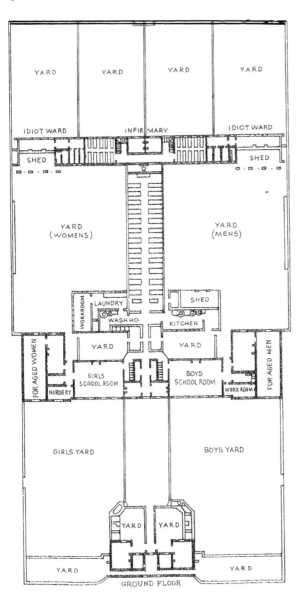

4 Plan of work-
house ground floor

any broken hats or petticoats, there were also stated hours and rules
thoroughly disgusting to the Celtic mind, and lastly, for the women,
there were caps without borders![4]

On admission entrants were assigned to the quarters appropriate to their
class. Inmates were initially divided into five classes – males and females of

13 years and over, boys and girls from five to 12 years and children under five years. The regulations provided that each class 'shall remain in the apartment assigned to them, without communication with any other class'. Separate accommodation and exercise yards were provided for each category so that families were isolated. This was rigorously observed. In 1848 the visiting committee recommended that the wall of the female yard be raised and a separate straw shed be built in the male yard so as to 'prevent all intercourse with the females which exists at present as a result of having only one straw house'. Mothers of children under five were permitted to have access to them at reasonable times. Guardians could make regulations subject to the approval of the commissioners for 'occasional interviews' by family members. Breaking up of families in this way was a deliberate policy to make the workhouses as unattractive as possible.[5]

Things improved slightly in 1843 when amended regulations defined adults as above the age of fifteen years.[6] Children under two years were then allowed remain with their mother if she desired it, children from two to seven years, when not in school, were in a special apartment to which mothers had access at all reasonable times. No able-bodied inmate could leave without taking his family with him. Any who did so were charged with leaving the family to be a burden on the union and a number of such cases are recorded in the minutes. In September 1851 sentences of one month and two months in prison for family desertion were noted in the minutes.

DISCIPLINE

The regulations provided that hours of rising, retiring, work and meals were to be at such times as the board would determine subject to the approval of the commissioners and these hours were marked by the ringing of a bell. A roll was called half an hour after the rising bell. The paupers were inspected before breakfast to ensure that each was in a 'clean and proper state'. Meals had to be eaten in silence and decorum maintained. Alcohol or tobacco was not allowed unless by written direction of the medical officer. Cards or games of chance were not permitted. No visitors were allowed except by permission of the master and in the presence of the master, matron or porter. The master and matron were required to inspect the wards at nine o'clock at night and see that all were in bed and lights and fires extinguished. The master was obliged to enforce order, punctuality, cleanliness and observance of the rules. The porter was required to assist in preserving order and in enforcing obedience as well as ensuring that no unauthorised person entered or left. He was required to examine all parcels and goods to prevent the admission of any liquor or food.

Anyone neglecting to observe the rules, using obscene language, refusing to work, wasting or wilfully damaging property of the union, making noise when silence was ordered was deemed 'disorderly' and placed in a special apartment and given such diet as the guardians would direct. Anyone repeating the offence within seven days or insulting an officer or found guilty of drunkenness or indecency was deemed 'refractory' and was punished by 'confinement and reduction in diet until taken before a justice of the peace'. Children under 12 could not be confined in a dark room or at night. Boys under fifteen could be given corporal punishment but girls were exempt from this form of punishment.[7]

In May 1842 the master was directed to maintain a punishment book recording the nature of offences, age and sex of the offender and the punishment imposed. The minutes record several instances of paupers brought before the board and admonished for refusing to work and the master was authorised to dismiss any repeat offenders. There are instances of boys being flogged for leaving the workhouse without permission, disobeying orders, absence from work, using insulting language to the teacher and for general insubordination.

EMPLOYMENT

As the name workhouse implies all inmates capable of work were obliged to do so. The principle was that 'the paupers shall be employed in the workhouse in any work which may be needed, and of which they may be capable, for the benefit of the union'.[8] The views of the commissioners on suitable employment were expressed as follows:[9]

> Male paupers are for the most part elderly, and more or less infirm, though most of them are able to do something; and with a view to keeping such of them from idleness as are not engaged in stone breaking, oakum-picking, cultivating the garden, or household work, a hand-mill has been provided for the use of the establishment, and other means will be resorted to as time and opportunity serve.
>
> For female inmates there is less difficulty in finding employment, the ordinary occupations of the establishment, joined with making and mending linen, knitting stockings, picking oakum, attending children and sick have furnished occupation for the far greater number of them.

The master was required to ensure that able-bodied adults were employed during the whole of the hours of labour, to train the youth in such employment as would best fit them for gaining their own living, to keep the partially disabled paupers occupied to the extent of their ability and to allow none who were capable of work to be idle at any time. Within the first month of opening the master was directed to employ any of the inmates capable of work in 'dressing the yards and grounds' and tools for breaking stones were ordered. Even children were expected to work some hours and in May 1841 the guardians decided to order ten hundredweight of old ropes in order to employ the boys and girls in picking oakum. This consisted of unravelling old ropes so that the fibres could be used in a preparation for sealing ships' timbers.

DIET

Within a week of opening the master reported that the diet was not sufficient for the male paupers and it was decided to allow an additional half-pound of potatoes and a half pint of milk each day. A month later an additional ounce of meal was allowed for breakfast but the commissioners objected. It was then decided to appoint a committee to examine the diets of the North Dublin and South Dublin Unions. Having considered the committee's report the board decided in June 1841 that breakfast should consist of a quart of stirabout made of eight ounces of oatmeal and to give a pound of bread and a pint of buttermilk instead of stirabout on Sundays. In November 1842 the master reported that Assistant Commissioner Hancock ordered him to cease providing this breakfast on Sundays. The board recorded their annoyance at this interference in the following terms 'such interference on the part of Mr Hancock was uncalled for and uncourteous (*sic*) of the board and master to be directed to continue bread and milk on Sundays'.

On the first Christmas Day bread, butter and coffee were given for breakfast and beef and extra potatoes for dinner and this practice was repeated in subsequent years. In March 1842 it was decided to give able-bodied paupers a pound of mutton on Easter Sunday and a half-pound to each child. The commissioners wrote to the board saying they observed this proposal 'with regret' and such a course was 'directly opposed to sound principle, and must tend to make the condition of the pauper superior to that of the industrious labourers, very many of whom will be unable to partake of such indulgence, although they are compelled to contribute towards the maintenance of the paupers in the workhouse'.[10] They requested the guardians to reconsider and the decision was reversed by five votes to four at the next meeting.

In February 1842 the board decided to give washerwomen a half-pound of bread on washday in addition to the normal diet. An objection from the commissioners was discussed at the following meeting when the minutes record that the guardians considered 'this duty fell much more severely on the paupers in this union than in the Dublin workhouses from the small number competent to perform the work'. It was resolved not to alter the decision. In 1848 the auditor criticised an allowance of supper to washer-women without the prior sanction of the commissioners. The board considered the women would not be able to do this work on the ordinary diet but their application to the commissioners for approval was rejected. Some time later a male pauper who was acting as barber applied for extra rations because of occasional work in the fever hospital. The board were sympathetic and applied to the commissioners for sanction and included in the application another request on behalf of the washerwomen. Extra food for the barber was approved but the commissioners refused to relent on the question of supper for the washerwomen.

EDUCATION

Great importance was attached by the commissioners to the training of children in moral and religious habits and fitting them by education and by careful instruction in useful branches of industry to earn their own liveli-hood and become respectable members of the community.[11] At least three hours of instruction were required every day for boys and girls in reading, writing and the Christian religion. In 1843 arithmetic and 'such other instruction as shall fit them for service' was added to the curriculum. The commissioners arranged with the National Board of Education to supply workhouse schools with books and other requisites without charge and further supplies at half price.[12] In return the schools had to be open to inspection by the Education Board.

In June 1841 the union advertised for a schoolmistress trained on the national system of education at a salary of £15 per annum and Hannah Fanning was appointed. In August an application was made to the Commis-sioners of Education for six dozen schoolbooks, four dozen table books, four dozen slates, one dozen scripture books, 1000 stone pencils and 100 quills. By 30 September 1844 there were 81 pupils in the school and two teachers.[13] By 30 September 1847 the number of pupils had increased to 307.[14] In March 1851, ten years after opening, pupil numbers had reduced to 210. In 1850 a female teacher named Magee was awarded a special gratuity of £2 10s. od. by the Commissioners of Education under a special scheme introduced to improve the quality of teaching in the workhouse schools.[15] In May 1851 the following report of the district inspector is recorded in the minutes:

> The teachers are rather well qualified as regards both their literary acquirements and method of conducting the school. The school has improved since my last inspection. In the female department the children of fourth and third class, particularly the former, are excellent readers, the children carefully exercised in the meanings of words and spell well in both schools. They have also improved in writing, particularly in the female department. They are very well trained and conduct themselves remarkably well.

From the early days a tailor and shoemaker were employed for the purpose of instructing the children in these trades and save the expense of making clothes and shoes. A salary of £7 10s. 0d. with rations was paid to each. On 25 February 1845, however, only two boys were learning a trade, one shoemaking and one tailoring.[16] This contrasts poorly with other workhouses in the area – in Rathdown 33 boys were apprenticed, 16 in Dunshaughlin, and 15 in Kells.[17] In February 1846 the tailor was dismissed for refusing to teach the children his trade. A replacement was appointed and a month later the master was able to report that he had sent three boys to work with the tailor and one with the shoemaker. In November 1848 the number of apprentices in shoemaking and tailoring was increased to eight in each category and these apprentices attended school half time.

Early in 1849 the board leased 14 Irish acres opposite the workhouse from Lord Howth at £2 per statute acre. The purpose was to give the boys a proper knowledge of agriculture along with their general education so as to enable them to get employment as 'at present they are being brought up in a most deplorable state of ignorance for want of agricultural education which is the only one suited to their sphere and future prospects'. A quarter acre was reserved for use as a burial ground – previously burials had taken place in the workhouse grounds. The remainder was sown with carrots, parsnips, mangolds, and turnips to provide food for the workhouse, oats to provide both food and straw, and flax seed in order to provide useful employment for the able-bodied female paupers.

The board appointed a Mr McCaffrey as agricultural manager at a salary of £30, a room and the same rations as the master. He was required to lecture on agricultural subjects to the male paupers each evening. The master was instructed to enforce discipline on those employed under him. Boys who refused to attend the lecture were deprived of milk and placed in solitary confinement. In August 1849, however, the board decided that while McCaffrey might have the theory to manage the farm he had not shown 'practical knowledge or energetic resolution in the management of the paupers and the cropping of the land'. The farm was placed under the direction of the master and McCaffrey was dismissed.

RELIGION

The regulations required that divine service be performed every Sunday but no pauper was compelled to attend any service contrary to his religious principles. Morning and evening prayers were recited by staff and grace before and after meals.

Revd Tyrrell, parish priest of Lusk, was appointed chaplain to the workhouse. His request for various articles required for his ministry was referred

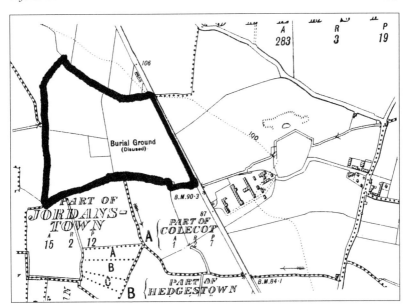

5 Map showing location of workhouse, farm and burial ground

to the commissioners. They approved provision of an altar, vestments, altar cloths, missal, candlesticks, chalice and crucifix at a total cost of £23. Later his request for 50 prayer books and 150 catechisms was also approved. No church building was provided in the early years but part of the dining hall was partitioned for use for religious services.

The salary payable to chaplains gave rise to controversy. The commissioners considered that chaplains should be paid at the same rates as in England. The Catholic chaplains argued that their duties were much more onerous than those of Church of England chaplains and the hierarchy became involved in correspondence with the commissioners. In November 1841 a scale was agreed for the larger workhouses and chaplains to houses with less than 600 inmates were to be paid in accordance with the special circumstances pertaining in each case.[18] Revd Tyrrell then wrote to the board saying he had been advised by the assistant commissioner to claim £25 per annum but that 'it was quite out of the question for him to take on the arduous duties at such a salary'. Matters dragged on until April 1842 when it was agreed that Revd Tyrrell would receive a salary of £40 per annum and Revd Potterton, chaplain of the established church, £26. Revd Tyrrell was arrested in October 1843 for involvement in the repeal movement and died on 4 December 1843 from 'illness produced by his prosecution and exertions for liberty'.[19]

In July 1842 the board agreed to order 24 yards of white muslin at a cost of 8*d.* per yard so that dresses could be made for the girls for confirmation

and to get twelve caps for the boys at 6*d*. each. A letter from the commissioners disapproving of this was read at the next meeting. The reaction of the
guardians is not recorded but as the muslin and caps do not appear in the
weekly list of goods ordered it seems that the children were confirmed in
their workhouse garb.

The religion of foundling children was a matter of controversy. The law
decreed that if the religion of the parents of any child admitted to the
workhouse was not known the child should be reared in the religion of the
state. Any attempt to change a child's registered religion had to be approved
by the board. There are a number of such incidents in the minutes, the first
in December 1841 when two of the Catholic guardians proposed that a
child be registered as a Catholic, as she had been found in a Catholic district
and taken in charge by a Catholic woman. Subsequently at the insistence of
the churchwarden the child was brought to the Protestant clergyman,
baptised by him and maintained for a year 'by a county presentment to the
minister and churchwarden'. Some time later the child was baptised by a
Catholic priest. Messrs Hamilton and Cobbe tried to have the matter
referred to the commissioners but were defeated in a vote and the child was
registered as Catholic.

HEALTH

What was described as 'fever' was a problem in the workhouse from the
start. As early as June 1841 there was insufficient accommodation in the
workhouse hospital for fever patients and a temporary hospital was opened
in Balbriggan to accommodate 24 fever patients. A medical attendant, master,
nurse and assistant nurse were appointed there. In February 1842 that hospital was reported to be full and some fever patients had to be kept in the
workhouse. Later that year work was started on a permanent fever hospital
in the workhouse grounds. This hospital with accommodation for 48 patients
was completed in 1845 at a cost of £397 and was financed by a loan from
the Bank of Ireland.[20] In 1847 a further building described as convalescent
wards was erected adjoining the fever hospital.

4. Administration and finance

The total number of guardians was 30 but attendance at the weekly board meetings was very low especially in the period 1841 to 1846. The following table shows the average attendance for each period for which minutes are available:

Table 4.1 Average attendance at board meetings

Period	Ex-officio guardians	Elected guardian	Average total attendance
May 1839–March 40	3	14	17
Apr 1840–March 41	3	11	14
Apr 1841–March 42	2	5	7
Apr 1842–Feb 43	2	5	7
Aug 1844–March 45	2	3	5
Sept 1845–March 46	2	3	5
Apr 1846–Sept 46	2	2	4
Apr 1848–March 49	3	5	8
Apr 1849–March 50	3	9	12

After the opening of the workhouse the attendance dropped markedly. One ex-officio guardian elected in 1839 and two elected in 1840 never attended a meeting. Even meetings to strike the rate never attracted more than 15 members. Attendance did not increase until 1848 when the expenses of the union had reached crisis point but even then never exceeded half the membership, apart from one occasion in 1849 when the post of clerk was to be filled and an attendance of 28 was recorded.

In the early days relations between the guardians and the commissioners were harmonious. On 19 April 1841, one month after opening, Assistant Commissioner Hall wrote to the board apologising that because of pressure of business he had been unable to attend meetings for some time. He added 'I have remarked with the utmost pleasure that the business has been conducted in my absence entirely to the satisfaction of the commissioners'. Relations soon deteriorated and over the years there were many clashes between the board and the commissioners who kept a very close eye on the activities of each union by a careful scrutiny of the minutes and interfered in the most routine matters. It was obligatory to send a copy of the minutes to the commissioners after each meeting, which immediately alerted them if actions of which they disapproved were contemplated.

The first clash occurred in July 1841 when it was decided to admit James Moore and four children although he had a house and garden in Swords and a wife living there. This decision was criticised by the commissioners who directed the board to:

> Pay serious attention to the evils that must ensue if the great principle of affording relief only to persons in a state of destitution be not closely adhered to. A man in possession of a house and garden cannot be said to be destitute, although he may be in indigent circumstances, and when to this it is added that he has a wife, of all of whose means he is by law entitled to avail himself, the commissioners cannot avoid concluding that, in this case, the sound principle has been departed from.

This was the first such case to come to their attention and they feared it would set a precedent.[1] The board adhered to their decision and directed the clerk to inform the commissioners that they 'were fully aware of the regulations for the admission of paupers and that they paid particular attention to the case but could not enter into the detail of evidence brought before them in each case'. In February and March 1842 the guardians were rebuked over the additional diet given to the washerwomen and the Easter Sunday lunch. The commissioners made these rebukes public by including the correspondence in their annual report.[2] The rent of the site was another contentious issue. In November 1841 the clerk was directed to write to the commissioners expressing surprise at the 'enormous and extravagant' rent that the board considered was at least 50 per cent above its value. In March 1842 Assistant Commissioner Phelan complained that he had been unable to audit the accounts due to their bad state and the board were obliged to employ a 'competent person' to put the accounts in order. A further confrontation occurred in November 1842 with Assistant Commissioner Hancock's order regarding Sunday breakfast.

Friction between boards of guardians and the commissioners was countrywide. In 1842 Daniel O'Connell spoke in the House of Commons of the 'flippancy and impertinence of their expressions and the determination, too, that they would not yield to local feelings and circumstances but maintain their own cast-iron system'.[3]

In March 1842 George Hamilton was elected chairman and was the most important figure in union affairs for the remainder of the decade. He held the post of chairman until 1850 apart from the year 1845 when the Hon St. John Butler was elected. In 1842 Hamilton was elected Member of Parliament for Dublin University after a number of unsuccessful attempts to be elected for Co. Dublin.

6 Portrait of
George Hamilton

In 1844 the commissioners amended the regulations governing poor law unions. One of the changes that caused annoyance throughout Ireland was the transfer from the guardians to the commissioners of the power to suspend the clerk. Letters conveying motions of protest were received in Balrothery from over 20 other unions. In November George Hamilton wrote to the board regretting that other public duties prevented him from attending as often as a chairman should – he had not attended the weekly meetings since 11 August. In his letter he stated in relation to the poor relief system:[4]

> Having since its enactment felt it my duty to endeavour by every means in my power, to render it as salutary and efficient as possible, it is with great regret I have observed an unceasing feeling of dissatisfaction in many parts of Ireland as regards the administration of the system. This dissatisfaction has now become so strong and so extensive as in my opinion to endanger imminently the system itself unless means be taken promptly and decisively by Government or Parliament to enquire into the causes of such a feeling and to remove them if possible. I attribute the dissatisfaction partly to defects in the system itself, which may require legislation to remove, but in greater degree to the virtually irresponsible position in which the commissioners are placed and to the course of policy which they and their assistants have adopted towards those upon whom mainly the beneficial working of the system must depend.
>
> I think as independent men and Irishmen anxious to sustain a measure intended for the relief of the Irish poor it is our duty to call

upon Parliament and Government to institute such an enquiry as will
be calculated to trace out causes of the present discontent, to lead to
the improvement of the system and its administration, and to render it
efficient for the purpose it was designed.

The board passed a unanimous resolution that a petition be prepared for
presentation to parliament and the petition was adopted two weeks later.
Early in 1846 a select committee of the House of Lords was established to
enquire into the operation of the poor laws and medical charities in Ireland
in response to several petitions. George Hamilton gave evidence to the
committee on 19 June 1846 and spoke of the animosity existing between
boards of guardians throughout Ireland and the central board in London
whose whole approach, he said, was at variance with the feelings of local
administrations. The views of guardians were ignored and there was no right
of appeal against the decisions of the commissioners.[5] The arrangement of
electoral districts and the inequality of rates that resulted were also causes of
grievance. The complaints regarding the central board in London were
answered in 1847 when an independent commission was established for
Ireland under the Poor Law Extension act of that year.

There was a heavy turnover of staff in the early years. Within two months
of opening the matron died of fever. Both Durnin (the master) and the
medical attendant were reprimanded by the board for failing to fumigate the
premises and prevent infection. The clerk was reprimanded for failure to get
chloride of soda although instructed to do so the previous week. All were
warned that greater diligence and energy would be expected henceforth.
The wife of the master was then appointed matron.

In February 1842 the master reported that the schoolmistress had
disobeyed him. No details are given but the board decided she should be
admonished for disobeying a reasonable order. In July the schoolmistress
retaliated by making a complaint against the master. The board investigated
and the master was warned he should not absent himself from the house
without the express permission of the board, that he should personally
supervise the weighing and distribution of provisions and visit the wards at
night. He was also warned to moderate his language and be extremely
cautious in his use of alcohol.

In October 1842 the vice-chairman reported that he and Assistant
Commissioner Hall had inspected the dormitories and found a great number
of tins filled with milk, potatoes, bread and in one instance meat. He said
that this showed that the master had ignored the order made by the board
forbidding the removal of food from the dining-hall and demonstrated 'great
neglect on the part of the master and the paupers in charge of the wards'.
He recommended that the master be dismissed if he was not much stricter
in future in supervising the workhouse.

The minutes from February 1843 to August 1844 are missing but some time during this period Durnin left. He and his wife were replaced by a Mr and Mrs Carroll. In October 1844 Durnin wrote to the guardians making accusations against Mr and Mrs Carroll. Following investigation the board decided that while there were some grounds for complaint for neglect in locking up the paupers they were not of a serious nature and a reprimand was sufficient. In December a report was made that the yards were filthy but again the master escaped with a warning that if it recurred he would be dismissed.

Kennelly, the first clerk, left some time between February and November 1843, as that month a Francis Carey was signing correspondence as clerk.[6] The reason for Kennelly's departure is not known but in view of the complaint of the assistant commissioner in March 1842 about the state of the accounts it is possible he was dismissed. His replacement did not last long. In the commissioners' tenth annual report a return appears in relation to paupers in workhouses giving details of previous occupations, age, marital status, number of children, state of health on admission and religion.[7] Balrothery is one of only four unions that failed to send a return. This is an unfortunate omission as this information is not now available from any other source. A return of salaries of union officers was published in 1843 and here also Balrothery is one of five unions from which no return was received.[8] In September 1844 the commissioners wrote to the board recommending Carey's resignation for failure to attend to his duties. The board in a rather tetchy reply regretted that their clerk was not satisfactory to the commissioners but they were not prepared to accept his resignation without a further trial. He departed, however, prior to April 1846 as Daly, the schoolmaster who had been appointed in March 1845, was then combining the posts of clerk and schoolmaster.

The board recognised that the workhouse was not being managed efficiently as on 24 February 1845 the clerk was directed to write to each guardian earnestly requesting them to visit the workhouse in turn one day per week, apart from the board meeting day, in order to 'check irregularities now existing in the house'. There is no evidence to show whether this was implemented.

A serious incident occurred in March 1845 when the nurse reported that the master had tried to take 'improper liberties' with her in a storeroom. On being called before the board Carroll admitted this but said he did not intend to harm her but had heard that she was an 'improper character and he wanted to try her'. He resigned immediately. Probably in retaliation his wife reported shortly afterwards that the porter was visiting the hospital and taking tea with the nurse. Both the porter and the nurse were strongly censured by the board and warned that if the visits continued both would be dismissed. The guardians were willing to let Mrs Carroll continue as matron but the commissioners refused to sanction this as they considered the retention of a matron after her husband resigned 'always led to much inconvenience'. In July 1845 the commissioners made an order dismissing Mrs Carroll as unfit for office.[9]

Martin Hogan was appointed master in April 1845. In October that year it was recorded in the minutes that 'everything in the workhouse was clean and most satisfactorily attended to, the food wholesome, the inmates clean and orderly, the matron and master appear to attend strictly to their duties'. Again in September 1846 the minutes note everything was in good order 'as had been the case since the arrival of the new master'. Hogan served until May 1851 when, much to the regret of the board, he left to take up a position in another union.

In April 1846 Daly, who some time previously had taken on the duties of clerk in addition to those of schoolmaster, was in serious trouble. The board found he had used for his own purposes a draft for £10 intended to enable the master to buy milk. He was absent for two days without permission and was accused of omitting to read the part of the master's report concerning himself. As the power to discipline a clerk was then vested in the commissioners the board requested an enquiry but Daly resigned. Seven applications were received for the vacancy of clerk and a Mr Kelly was appointed who remained until his death in August 1849. In April 1849 the board noted his absence due to illness and testified to his great efficiency and attention to duty. Daly's replacement as schoolmaster, a Mr Dowdall, was dismissed as unfit in November 1849.[10]

There was difficulty filling the vacancy caused by the death of Kelly. The first man appointed was asked to resign in March 1850, five months after taking up duty, because of his inefficiency. He left leaving large arrears of work 'which caused great confusion and irregularity in the proceedings of the board'. The next man, Robert Graham, who had been elected at a meeting on 1 May 1850 attended by the exceptionally large number of 28 guardians, withdrew when it was alleged he had attended an Orange procession in Cootehill on 12 July 1849 wearing an orange scarf.[11] The next appointment, a Mr Connell, had a testimonial from the chairman, George Hamilton, but the commissioners refused to sanction his appointment. Some of the board considered the attitude of the commissioners unreasonable on the grounds that the assistant commissioner put a question to Connell 'when he was in a nervous state after election requiring a far-fetched fraction of 2/79'. They decided, however, that they would not object if the commissioners required him to undergo an examination. The following letter dated 19 June 1850 from Connell to the commissioners appears in the minutes of 3 July:

I believe that in numerous instances it must have come under your observation that where a clerk was elected who never performed the duties of the office no objection has ever been made to his employing a qualified and competent person for the purpose of assisting him. This I intend to do at my own expense. I can procure the services of an eminent person who was for many years clerk in a workhouse and if after a trial I do not find myself perfectly competent I will resign and pay all expenses of the election of a new clerk. I think it so reasonable and only just to me and the guardians who elected me that I should have a fair trial and I feel sure her majesty's commissioners will not refuse it.

Not surprisingly this was unacceptable to the commissioners. In the interim the master, Hogan, acted as clerk. As the minute book for the next nine months is missing it is not possible to learn any further developments in this episode but in August 1851 a Robert Scallon was appointed clerk.

In the first ten years the turnover in the two key posts of clerk and master was high – six persons held the post of clerk and three that of master. Only one in each category proved efficient and able for the demands of the job – Hogan who was master from April 1845 until May 1851 and Kelly who was clerk from 1845 to August 1849.

FINANCE

The expenses for the period March 1841 to September 1850 were as follows:

Table 4.2 Expenses, March 1841 to September 1850

March 1841 to 29 Sept. 1841	£1,320
Year ended 29 Sept. 1842	£1,654
Year ended 29 Sept. 1843	£1,309
Year ended 29 Sept. 1844	£1,532
Year ended 29 Sept. 1845	£2,652
Year ended 29 Sept. 1846	£2,315
Year ended 29 Sept. 1847	£4,055
Year ended 29 Sept. 1848	£5,477
Year ended 29 Sept. 1849	£5,943
Year ended 29 Sept. 1850	£5,152

Source: Annual Reports of the Poor Law Commissioners, 1841–1850.

Revenue was raised by means of a tax on property known as the poor rate and was payable in equal parts by the occupier and landlord, unlike the county cess which was levied solely on occupiers. Because of the difficulty of collecting rates from smallholders occupiers of all holdings valued at four pounds and under were relieved in 1843 of the obligation to pay rates, the full rates becoming payable by the lessor.[12] In the Balrothery Union 1898 persons, or 41 per cent of the total number occupying land, were exempted by this measure.[13] These people had occupied 594 statute acres or approximately one third of an acre each.[14]

The first rate, made in December 1840, was five pence in the pound in every electoral district. Three rate collectors were employed and were remunerated by means of a percentage of the amount collected. In October 1841 two of the collectors, when summoned to the board because of the unsatisfactory state of the collection, said several refused to pay and they could not enforce payment without recourse to 'distress' or seizure and sale of goods. This is the only reference in the minutes to resistance to payment of rates. At the end of 1841 the sum of £242 (12½ per cent) was uncollected.[15] In April 1842 the minutes record that two of the collectors had not used 'due diligence', one was deemed unfit to be re-appointed and the other declined re-appointment.

After 1841 a separate rate was made for each electoral district as each area was responsible for its own poor. Table 4.3 shows the rate struck for each electoral district between 1842 and 1850 and illustrates the huge increase from 1847 onwards:

Table 4.3 Rate made each year from 1842 to 1851[16]

District	1842	1843	1844	1845	1846	1847	1848	1849	1850	1851
	s. d.	s. d.	s. d.	s. d.	s. d.	s. d.	s. d.	s. d.	s. d.	s. d.
Balbriggan	0. 7½	0.10	1. 0	1. 0	0. 9	2. 5	1. 6	2. 0	1.10	2.1½
Balscadden	0. 2½	0. 2½	0. 2	0. 4	0. 5	1. 8	1. 2	1. 6	1. 4	1. 6
Holmpatrick	0. 2½	0. 5	0. 4	0. 7	0. 8	1.11	0. 10	1. 6	1. 6	1.5½
Lusk	0. 5	0. 5	0. 4	0. 7	0. 6	2. 0	1. 4	2. 0	1. 8	2. 0
Ballyboughal	0. 2½	0. 2½	0. 2	0. 5	0. 5	0. 7	0. 8	1. 0	1. 2	1. 2
Hollywood	0. 2½	0. 2½	0. 2	0. 6	0. 8	1. 4	0. 8	1. 6	1. 3	1. 5
Clonmethan	0. 2½	0. 5	0. 3	0. 5	0. 6	0.11	0. 6	1. 3	1. 4	1. 3
Swords	0. 5	0. 7½	0. 4	0. 4	0. 9	1.11	0. 8	1. 3	1.10	1. 11
Kilsallaghan	0. 2½	0. 5	0. 2	0. 3	0. 5	1. 0	0. 8	0. 6	1. 2	1.5½
Donabate	0. 2½	0. 5	0. 4	0. 3	0. 6	1. 2	0. 4	1. 0	1. 6	1. 1
Kinsealy	0. 5	0. 7½	0. 4	0. 5	0. 8	1. 1	0. 4	1. 3	1. 3	1. 3
Malahide	0. 2½	0. 2½	0. 2	0. 4	0. 6	0. 5	0. 4	1. 8	1. 6	1. 3

Throughout the decade Balbriggan was consistently rated highest, indicating that the largest numbers obtaining relief came from that district. In most areas the rate increase in 1847 was enormous and the impact on farmers must have been extremely severe. In April 1848 the board were advised by the commissioners that they considered the rate struck in some areas was insufficient. The board, however, decided not to make a new rate as there were substantial arrears from 1847. Rates had to be maintained at a high level in the years 1849, 1850 and 1851. In 1849 'Rate-in-Aid' was imposed requiring all unions in Ireland to contribute to the support of distressed unions in the west and south by means of a special rate of six pence in the

NOTICE

That a Rate has been Made.

BALROTHERY UNION.

ELECTORAL DIVISIONS OF
Swords and Kinsealy.

I HEREBY GIVE NOTICE that a Rate of Seven Pence Half-penny in the Pound, for the Relief of the Poor, has been duly made on the Property situated in the above mentioned Electoral Divisions, Rateable under the provisions of the 1*st* and 2*nd Vic., Cap.* 56, and that the said Rate was this day signed at a Board of Guardians, and is now in my custody, and may be seen at the Board Room, on any day, except Sundays, between the hours of Ten o'Clock in the forenoon, and 4 o'Clock in the afternoon.

Signed this 27th day of December, 1842.

JAMES KENNELLY,

Clerk of the Union.

By Authority—A. THOM, 86, Abbey-street, Dublin.

7 Notice dated December 1842

pound. On 26 March 1849 George Hamilton speaking in the House of Commons against this proposal said 'small farmers could ill afford to make any payment, in many cases this additional six pence would have the effect of reducing a struggling union to pauperism'.[17] The government was determined, however, that Irish property would pay for Irish poverty and all opposition to the measure was in vain. The Chief Poor Law Commissioner, Edward Twistleton, resigned in protest at this failure to make the distress in Ireland a charge on the United Kingdom as a whole. On 25 April 1849 the board of Balrothery Union passed a resolution recording their admiration for his stand. They described his resignation as a 'singular instance of public virtue' and regretted that 'at so important a crisis Ireland should be deprived of the services of a gentleman so eminent and patriotic'.

Between January and June 1849 the numbers in the workhouse were at the highest level ever, averaging 587 per week, with a further weekly average of 41 and 69 in the workhouse and fever hospitals. In January 1850 the expenditure for the coming year was estimated at £5,940, Rate-in-Aid amounted to £2,367, repayments of the loan for operating soup kitchens in 1847 was £684, making a total of £5,940 to be raised, and in addition arrears of rates amounted to £2,595. Instalments on the loan for building the workhouse apparently had not been paid in the previous two years as a letter from the Public Works Loan Office calling for five instalments amounting to £1,475 was received at this time. Requests were coming weekly from other creditors for settlement of accounts – the minutes of 24 April 1850 refer to 'applications from many other parties to whom large sums are due'. An unsuccessful approach was made to Lord Howth to abate the rent on the site. A deputation was sent to the Bank of Ireland to negotiate a loan of £1,500 for six months. On 1 May the deputation was directed to approach the bank again to borrow £500 for six months, the interest to be paid by private subscription of the guardians. These loans enabled payment of bills totalling £2,000 in the following month. At the end of June 1850 the sum of £5,396 was still uncollected and one of the contractors to the workhouse was threatening to withhold supplies if payment was not made more regularly. In December 1850 the government imposed Rate-in-Aid once more, this time at 2*d*. in the pound.

In April 1851 when the next available minute book commences the amount outstanding had reduced to £2,963. The road to financial solvency, however, had still some way to go. On 9 April 1851, ten years after opening there were still 548 in the workhouse, 35 in the workhouse hospital and 30 in the fever hospital causing continuing heavy running costs. With these financial burdens it is not surprising that on 22 October 1851 the visiting committee reported to the board 'there were many deficiencies in the work-house which require attention but in the present unsatisfactory financial state of the union it appears premature to enter into any further detail'.

5. The Famine years

The minutes of 29 October 1845 provide the first reference to failure of the potato crop when the master reported he had bought potatoes which appeared good but when boiled were totally unfit for use. At the following meeting a letter from the commissioners authorising an alternative diet was noted. At this stage three-quarters of the potato crop in the Balrothery Union had been lost. This information is contained in letters sent to the Mansion House Committee in November 1845 by both the board and the parish priest of Balbriggan.[1]

The number in the workhouse rose steadily, from 200 in October 1845 to 336 on 5 June 1846 and then declined during the summer months. There is no other reference in the minutes to the prevailing situation until 18 March 1846 when a letter appeared in the *Freeman's Journal* from one of the guardians, Thomas Mathews, which caused consternation in the boardroom. Mr Mathews wrote that famine existed to an alarming extent throughout the entire union, but particularly in Balbriggan and Lusk which he represented, that the number in the workhouse was 100 more than at the same time last year and that there were 18 cases of typhoid fever. At the next meeting a resolution was passed denying that famine existed in the union. While recognising there were some individual cases of want, the guardians considered these could be relieved 'by a small extension of that inherent benevolence for which the many wealthy and respectable landholders of this union have been at all times so remarkable'. They ordered immediate application to the Grand Jury to appoint special road sessions in order to provide employment.

Mathews exaggerated somewhat as the number of inmates recorded in the minute book for 11 March 1846 was 280 and for 10 March 1845 was 238. He may have been correct concerning typhoid as the number of patients in the fever hospital rose to 18 at the end of February 1846 from an average of two patients each week in the previous four months. He wrote as a politician might do today in stating in his letter 'it is most fortunate that we have a fever hospital here and I am happy for the reflection that after twelve months battling in the boardroom it was on my resolution that the hospital was built'. From his letter we learn that the price of lumpers – the cheapest variety of potatoes – had reached ten shillings a barrel in Balbriggan market and that only one barrel had been sent there in the previous five days. He also tells that Mr Hamilton had reduced his rents from £9 to £3, 'as did all the landlords with one exception, and supplied his tenants with turnips at little more than one penny per stone'.

From September 1846 following almost total failure[2] of a reduced potato crop – only 3,157 acres of potatoes were planted in 1846 compared with 5,527 acres in 1845[3] – the numbers seeking admission grew rapidly and on 12 December 1846 the workhouse was full.[4] As an economy measure the board decided to mix Indian meal with oatmeal for breakfast. Indian meal was one of the cheapest foods by which human life could be sustained. Although it could not be grown in Ireland it could be imported at considerably less cost than homegrown oatmeal.[5] The workhouse diet now consisted of stirabout for breakfast and bread for dinner.

By 2 January 1847 the number in the workhouse had reached 456.[6] The guardians were obliged to take emergency measures and introduced a form of outdoor relief by directing the master to provide a meal to any destitute persons seeking admission, before sending them away. They also decided to take a room or house in districts where destitution prevailed and provide meals of bread and soup or milk. This was reported in *The Times* on 11 January 1847 and was described as a 'bold step'.

Speaking in the House of Commons on 20 January 1847 George Hamilton said 'the general feeling in boards of guardians was that starvation must be prevented at whatever cost'.[7] He said he had summoned his board specially and proposed the opening of 'district rooms or houses' which was approved unanimously. This decision had not been favourably received by the commissioners and he criticised them for failing to act with the energy that 'so extraordinary an emergency required'. On 2 February he spoke on the state of the small farmer in his area whose 'slender comforts – the pig, the poultry, the household furniture – were disappearing under the slow but certain advance of this heavy calamity'.[8] This statement appears to be supported by the figures for articles pawned in Balbriggan. In 1845 a pawnbroking office was opened there and 9,702 articles were pawned that year, in 1846 the figure rose to 22,172 but in 1847 it fell to 15,641 possibly indicating that by 1847 many of the poor had nothing left to pawn.[9]

From the end of January 1847 to 1 May (the latest date for which figures in 1847 are available) there were over 500 in the workhouse reaching a peak of 547 in mid-April with a further 34 in the hospital and 15 in the fever hospital.[10] By 1 May accommodation for an additional 197 was provided by erecting sleeping galleries and appropriating officers' accommodation.[11] Further accommodation was provided later as in November 1847 the commissioners made an order authorising the board to borrow £600 to erect additional buildings in the workhouse grounds.[12] Figure 8 shows the average weekly numbers in the workhouse for each year for which records survive and makes clear that pressure on the workhouse continued until 1850.

During autumn 1846 local relief committees were formed. Funds raised by these committees were matched by the government-appointed Relief Commission. Early in October George Hamilton convened a meeting in

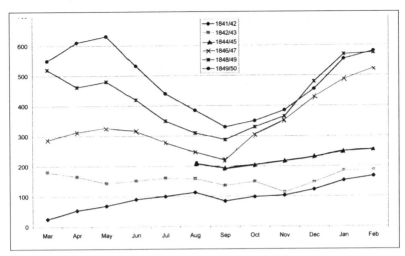

8 Graph showing average weekly number of residents, 1841–50

Balbriggan in order to establish a relief committee for the baronies of East and West Balrothery. The magistrates and others present pledged that they would endeavour to provide employment.[13] A week later an extraordinary presentment session of the Grand Jury for the barony of Nethercross was held at Swords when, in addition to the magistrates and nine cess payers, 'the courthouse was crowded with labourers and townspeople of the district'. The chairman, Charles Cobbe of Donabate, suggested they consider the number of men likely to be unemployed in the following four months and raise a sum sufficient to pay them for that period.[14]

A relief committee for the barony of Nethercross was also established in October 1846. A letter circulated to property and landowners requesting subscriptions for the purpose of establishing a depot for the sale of provisions at reduced rates survives.[15] This committee adopted the practice of issuing tickets redeemable with local traders in part payment for meal as they considered this the cheapest method of providing assistance. The Relief Commission wrote to the committee on 26 November 1846 saying that the issue of meal tickets without requiring work in return was contrary to government instructions, and the only exception was the infirm poor if the workhouse was full. The secretary replied that most recipients were employed on public works under the Board of Works and their remuneration at 14*d.* per day was totally inadequate to support a family. This appeal was rejected as an endorsement on the letter says 'gratuitous distribution in aid of wages not allowable'. The committee subsequently changed its practice as in January 1847 the list of subscriptions amounting to £305 was sent to the Relief Commission with a covering letter saying:

The committee operates over a very extensive agricultural district with few resident landlords to assist in alleviating the distress and destitution which prevails to an alarming degree. In the town and immediate neighbourhood of Swords there is a population of nearly 3,000 souls, a vast majority of which are in extreme want. The committee has established a soup kitchen at Swords and purchased a quantity of meal and rice, which we dispose of according to the Lord Lieutenant's instructions and give gratuitous relief only to such persons as are fit objects for the workhouse, but who for want of accommodation cannot be admitted. We have also purchased a quantity of woollen and cotton yarns and have a number of females employed in knitting stockings.

At end of December 1846 a relief committee was established for the district of Holmpatrick because of the distress in the town of Skerries. A soup kitchen was opened there on 1 January 1847 and tickets for soup and bread were distributed to 200 each day.[16] By the end of February 300 were being fed each day.[17] Work was not required in return as the Holmpatrick committee established a special fund and did not seek matching funds from the Relief Commission. On 18 January 1847 Eliza Taylor of Ardgillan wrote to her brother:

> I have nothing cheerful to tell you about the poverty and wretchedness of the poor people around us but everybody seems to be doing their best to assist them, even Mr Woods not content with the soup kitchen at Skerries has begun giving out soup at Milverton for his own poor. We became gradually so overwhelmed with beggars that there was no bearing the perpetual crowd of hungry naked creatures at the door.
>
> The board of works are culpably negligent about paying their men or providing sufficient number of pay clerks, from that cause arises the only bad feeling I have heard of in the neighbourhood. I really cannot blame the poor creatures when they become violent and insist on having money for food. On Saturday there was near being a serious outbreak in Balbriggan in consequence of there being no pay clerk. As usual poor Mr Hamilton stood in the gap.[18]

On 29 January 1847 Captain Robertson, agent for Sir Roger Palmer of Rush, wrote to the Relief Commission saying:

> It is not easy to convey an adequate description of the condition of this place and the amount of distress prevailing in it. The population of the village and its immediate neighbourhood is considerably above 3,000 souls. From it, crowds of individuals weekly throng the workhouse, applying for admission, but apply in vain, owing to the overflowing state of that establishment. The swarms of small landholders (some of roods

and half roods and even less) had hitherto very much depended for support by supplying the Dublin market with early potatoes. But the failure of that crop during the last two years has reduced them to poverty and abject distress.[19]

Contributions were given by individual landlords to the Grand Jury to assist in providing employment. Charles Cobbe of Donabate gave £40 to the district surveyor which the surveyor reported enabled him to employ several men in the vicinity of Swords.[20] George Hamilton, George Woods and 'other gentlemen connected to the baronies of East and West Balrothery' subscribed over £300 to provide employment in Balbriggan, Skerries, Rush and Lusk. The district surveyor described this as a most liberal contribution.[21]

In February 1847 the Temporary Relief act introduced soup kitchens, administered by poor law guardians and funded by government loans repayable from the poor rate. Local committees drew up lists of people requiring relief and this was the first outdoor relief allowed by the government without a work test. Soup kitchens were opened under this act in every electoral district except Malahide and the numbers fed daily are shown in table 5.1.

Table 5.1 Numbers fed, April–August 1847[22]

Electoral District and Date Relief Commenced		Max. Number Fed in One Day	Number on Relief List on 15 Aug. 1847	Amount of Loans Advanced	Amount of Donations	Total*
Balbriggan	5 April	507	240	–	£218	£218
Ballyboghal	25 April	35	25	£46	–	£46
Balscaddan	5 April	128	57	£88	–	£88
Clonmethan	12 May	45	35	£50	–	£50
Donabate	31 May	172	75	£81	–	£81
Hollywood	10 May	143	63	£77	–	£77
Holmpatrick	24 May	377	253	–	£65	£65
Kilsallaghan	7 June	83	23	£22	–	£22
Kinsealy	1 May	171	50	£114	–	£114
Lusk	21 June	819	237	£204	–	£204
Swords	9 June	921	255	–	£190	£190
Total		3401	1313	£682	£473	£1155

* Amount advanced by Relief Commissioners

This form of relief was terminated on 15 August 1847 by order of the government. At the peak of operations some 12 per cent of the population were fed daily. This varied from 25 per cent in Swords to 4 per cent in Ballyboghal. However, the percentage fed in the Balrothery union under this scheme was one of the lowest in the country – only Edenderry and the northern unions had lower figures.[23] In the adjoining unions of Dunsaughlin and Drogheda 36 per cent and 26 per cent of the population were assisted.

Blight re-appeared in 1847, on a smaller scale than in 1846, but because of the scarcity of seed potatoes a smaller crop had been sown and the total produce was nowhere more than a quarter of normal.[24] In autumn 1847 the Irish Poor Law Extension act introduced outdoor relief and placed the entire responsibility on boards of guardians. This act recognised the right to relief either in or out of the workhouse of certain categories, 1) destitute persons disabled by old age, infirmity or mental defect, 2) destitute persons unable to work because of ill health, 3) orphans and 4) destitute widows with two or more legitimate dependent children. The Poor Law Commissioners ordered that relieving officers be appointed in all unions at salaries of not less than £35 per annum, with powers to provide immediate and temporary relief in cases of sudden and urgent necessity.[25] One relieving officer per 12,000 population was recommended. A relieving officer was required to be 'a person of considerable influence in his district' as the guardians would be dependent to a considerable extent on his recommendations. The main characteristic required, in addition to the ability to read, write and keep accounts, was intelligence and firmness of mind so as to be able to resist intimidation in the discharge of his duties.[26]

The commissioners were vehemently opposed to granting outdoor relief to able-bodied men and described it as 'the evil which must be guarded against'.[27] If there was not sufficient room in the workhouse to accommodate able-bodied applicants the commissioners recommended that children and schoolteachers be moved to a separate establishment.[28] Any able-bodied persons receiving outdoor relief were required to give at least eight hours labour at a stone depot for each day's relief. The commissioners feared that without some rigid test outdoor relief would be liable to abuse and that stone breaking was more capable of effective supervision than any other form of labour.[29] Lists of those receiving relief both in and out of the workhouse were required to be posted every two weeks in each electoral district and at police stations. Anyone holding more than a quarter of an acre was obliged under the infamous Gregory clause to surrender his land before getting relief.[30]

The next available minute book commences on 31 March 1848 when six relieving officers were employed. An allowance of one pound of Indian meal per adult per day and half a pound to children under twelve was given as relief. There were then 872 persons receiving outdoor relief at a weekly cost of £20. In addition there were 520 in the workhouse, 37 in the hospital and 29 in the fever hospital.

In 1848 blight, as virulent as in 1846, re-appeared in many parts of the country.[31] In Co. Dublin yields were below 28 cwt per acre and were among the lowest in the country.[32] In November 1848 the guardians decided that depots should be opened for distribution of meal in Balbriggan, Skerries, Lusk, Rush, Donabate, Swords, Malahide and The Naul and these depots operated until 15 December 1849 when outdoor relief was terminated with the exception of the infirm and those over sixty years. This resulted in halving the numbers on outdoor relief and reducing the cost to approximately £10 per week. Outdoor relief for the elderly and infirm was continued until August 1850.

The regulation that any able-bodied person applying for relief enter the workhouse or if it was full labour at a stone depot for each day's outdoor relief was rigorously applied. There is evidence that men were put to work breaking stones as in April 1848 the guardians accepted an offer of one shilling and six pence per ton for broken stones. At the meeting of 3 January 1849 a letter was read on behalf of labourers from Swords. They were informed that outdoor relief could not be given to able-bodied persons but if they presented themselves at the workhouse they would be admitted. At the next meeting the master was instructed to make arrangements to have some of the old and infirm leave the workhouse and be given outdoor relief so as to make room for the able-bodied.

On 25 January 1849 the commissioners made an order limiting numbers in the workhouse to 620 and 100 in the fever hospital.[33] These limits, however, were exceeded for four weeks from 28 April to 19 May 1849 during the outbreak of cholera and peaked at 654 on 5 May.[34] This figure did not include the patients in the hospitals.

In January 1849 there was difficulty getting adequate supplies of milk and the board ordered rice-flour or cocoa to be substituted. In April the master reported insubordination and refusal to work by paupers due to the diet change. The visiting committee confirmed this reporting a 'universal complaint of the change in diet' and added 'in consequence of the mutiny now existing amongst paupers your committee suggest four ounces of bread be added at dinner as new milk cannot be procured'.

Conditions both for inmates and staff during these years must have been grim. Overcrowding was responsible for unhealthy conditions and would have contributed to the spread of disease. In April 1848 it was reported that the nursery because of its overcrowded state was 'often in a very unwholesome condition'. The workrooms were overcrowded in April 1849 and the lunatic cells were altered at a cost of £427 to provide additional workrooms. In December 1848 the inmates of the male infirm ward complained to the visiting committee of the cold and 'entreat an additional quantity of coal'. The response is not given in the minutes.

Sickness was a major problem in all workhouses and as late as February 1850 diarrhoea and dysentery were prevalent in the workhouse. In the ten years between 1841 and 1851 a total of 151 died in the workhouse from these famine-related diseases and a further 32 died from what is described simply as 'fever'.[35] The total number of deaths in the workhouse in that period was 778.[36] The death rate increased substantially in the period January to April 1847 (no figures are available from May 1847 to March

1848) and again in 1849 as can be seen from the following table. The figures have been taken from the minute books and parliamentary returns.

Table 5.2 Deaths in the workhouse, 1844–50

Period	Number of deaths	Average deaths per week
17 Aug 1844–28 Dec 1844	9	0.47
4 Jan 1845–12 April 1845	16	1.14
20 Sept 1845–27 Dec 1845	11	0.79
3 Jan 1846–19 Sept 1846	32	0.86
9 Jan 1847–1 May 1847	69	4.31
31 March 1848–30 Dec 1848	74	1.90
13 Jan 1849–25 Dec 1849	163	3.32
5 Jan 1850–29 June 1850	72	2.88

Cholera was reported in May 1849 in Balbriggan and spread quickly. The building previously used as a fever hospital in Balbriggan was opened as a cholera hospital and two medical attendants were appointed. Temporary cholera hospitals were also opened in Rush and Skerries[37] but until this was done some cholera cases had to be sent to the workhouse hospital. This led the guardians to require a new entry to the boardroom so as to avoid the risk of infection by passing the paupers on the stairs. By October 1849 the following statistics were recorded in the minutes:

Table 5.3 Number of cases and deaths from cholera, 1849

District	Number of cases	Number of deaths
Balbriggan	111	22
Holmpatrick	126	45
Lusk	846	171
Malahide	42	19
Swords	99	10
Total	1224	267

In addition 102 persons died in the workhouse from cholera.[38] In November a motion proposing to give the Catholic chaplain a gratuity of ten pounds in recognition of his increased workload during the cholera outbreak was defeated.

The Poor Law Acts empowered unions to assist emigration but there is no evidence that this was used until 1849 and then only on a limited scale. Ten girls were sent to Australia in 1849 under a government sponsored scheme[39] to send orphan girls aged between 14 and 18 years to Australia to help redress the gender imbalance in the colony. A group of 73 persons consisting of 28 males, 22 females and 23 children was sent to Quebec at the expense of the Swords electoral district and the sum of ten shillings was allowed to each for clothing on landing.[40] The passage of a woman and two children was paid to enable her to join her husband in India. In June 1850 two widows, one with five children and the other with four, were sent to Quebec.

The minutes from July 1850 to April 1851 are missing but on 9 April 1851, ten years after opening, the number in the workhouse was 548 exceeding the original capacity by more than one third. Included in this number were 37 able-bodied males, 94 able-bodied females and 244 children. In addition there were 35 in the workhouse hospital and 30 in the fever hospital. The presence of 131 able-bodied persons, bearing in mind the harshness of the regime, indicates that life still held no better option for many.

EFFECTS OF THE FAMINE

Population: The population of the union declined from 28,111 in the census of 1841 to 24,774 in the 1851 census or by 12 per cent. The decline occurred both in towns and rural districts:

Table 5.4A Population of major towns

Town	1841	1851	Decrease	Percentage Decrease
Swords	1,788	1,294	494	28
Balbriggan	2,959	2,310	649	22
Rush	1,603	1,496	107	7
Skerries	2,519	2,327	192	8

Table 5.4B Population of electoral districts

Electoral district	1841	1851	Change	Percentage Change
Balbriggan	4,881	3,864	-1,017	-21
Ballyboghal	842	705	-137	-16
Balscadden	1,074	892	-182	-17
Clonmethan	716	631	-85	-12
Donabate	1,170	1,160	-10	-1
Hollywood	1,927	1,546	-381	-20
Holmpatrick	4,338	4,549	+211	+5
Kilsallaghan	1,312	1,052	-260	-20
Kinsealy	1,267	1,113	-154	-12
Lusk	4,892	4,282	-610	-12
Malahide	2,059	2,018	-41	-2
Swords	3,633	2,962	-671	-18
Total	28,111	24,774	-3,337	-12

The only district to show an increase was Holmpatrick and this is accounted for by the location of the workhouse in that district – the census of 1851 records 556 in the workhouse. The decline in the Balrothery Union contrasts with the increase in the population of the county of Dublin by nearly 7,000 or by five per cent between 1841 and 1851. The population of

the Union of Rathdown in south Co. Dublin rose by some 5,500 or 16 per
cent while the population of the city of Dublin increased by 25,000 or 11
per cent. This rise in the city population is explained in the general report of
the 1851 census by the statement 'if famine visits the country, to supplement
their wants the rural population flood to the towns'. The residents of the
rural areas in the Balrothery Union did not flood to the towns in their own
district as is clear from Table 5.4A which shows the population of all towns
falling. The decline in population can only be explained by migration to the
city of Dublin, by emigration to England or further afield, and by deaths
from cholera and famine-related diseases.

Agriculture: The number of land holdings fell by 165 as shown in the
table below:

Table 5.5 Number of land holdings in 1841[41] and 1851[42]

Farm size	Number in 1841	Number in 1851
1 acre and less	677	620
1+ –5 acres	718	584
5+ –50 acres	1,011	1,066
50+ – 100 acres	218	205
100+ –200 acres	153	141
200+ –500 acres	64	62
500+ acres	4	2
Total	2,845	2,680

The number of holdings not exceeding one acre fell by a mere 57, while
holdings between one and five acres fell by 134. In 1841 the pattern of land
holdings in north Co. Dublin was fairly close to the national pattern in that
farms not exceeding five acres constituted 49 per cent of the total while the
national total for farms of this size was 45 per cent. By 1851 a huge change
had taken place in other parts and in 1851 farms of five acres and less
represented only 15 per cent of the total nationally. In north Co. Dublin
farms of this size still comprised 45 per cent of the total.

A comparison of the census of 1841 with that of 1851 shows that
dependence on agriculture altered during the decade. Occupations were
classified in three groups – families chiefly engaged in 1) agriculture, 2)
manufacture and trade and 3) other pursuits.

The pre-eminence of agriculture in 1841 is evident. The striking feature of
these figures, however, is the drop in 1851 in the number and percentage of
families engaged in agriculture and the corresponding increase in those engaged
in other pursuits. The total number of families decreased by 601. The number in
agriculture fell by 1,078 or almost one third to 2,230 and the numbers depend-

ent on manufacture and trade dropped by 168. Some of these found other occupations as the number in 'other pursuits' increased by 645. It appears, however, that the 601 families who disappeared were largely those in agriculture.

Families were also classified according to means –

1) Those chiefly dependent on vested means or professions. Farmers of more than fifty acres were included in this category.

2) Families living by the direction of labour. This was defined as 'heads of families with some fixed income or employment, also artisans who possess acquired capital in the knowledge of some trade, neither of which classes, however, is wholly exempt from labour. This may include farmers of five to fifty acres'.

3) Those dependent on their own manual labour. This included farmers of up to five acres.

4) Those whose means were not specified.

Table 5.6 Occupations of families in 1841 and 1851 classified by pursuits

Pursuits	1841	Percentage	1851	Percentage	Change
Agriculture	3,308	61	2,230	46	-1,078
Manufacture and trade	1,496	27	1,328	27	-168
Other	671	12	1,316	27	+645
Total families	5,475		4,874		-601

Table 5.7 Occupations of families in 1841 and 1851 classified by means

	1841	Percentage	1851	Percentage	Change
Vested means, professions	143	3	303	6	+160
Direction of labour	1,717	31	1,140	24	-577
Own manual labour	3,390	62	3,036	62	-354
Not specified	225	4	395	8	+170
Total families	5,475		4,874		-601

Between 1841 and 1851 the number of families with wealth or a profession or large farms increased by 160 and the number of families of unspecified means increased by 170. Families dependent on their own manual labour (including farmers with less than five acres) fell by 354 although their proportion of the total did not change. Families in the second category (artisans and farmers of five to 50 acres) declined by 577 indicating that with the addition of the 354 labourers and small farmers some 900 families disappeared from agriculture. Medium sized farmers would have been severely hit by the difficulties of the second half of the decade. Loss of the potato meant loss of food for animals as well as for humans and consequent drop in income. Andrew Kettle tells that livestock lived mainly on potatoes.[43] Farmers were obliged, in addition to paying rent for their farms, to pay poor rates, which increased drastically from 1847, and substantial county cess, which was levied only on occupiers. Figures for cess on a union basis are not available but its size can be judged from the figures for Co. Dublin between 1843 and 1849:[44]

Table 5.8 Amount of cess levied in Co. Dublin, 1843–1849

1843	£25,926
1844	£24,754
1845	£25,261
1846	£37,118
1847	£36,070
1848	£27,389
1849	£28,634

In 1849 and 1850 'Rate-in-Aid' for support of the distressed unions in the west and south of Ireland was added to their burden.

Housing: Both the 1841 and the 1851 census give details of housing accommodation. Existing houses were divided into four classes. Category four consisted of mud cabins of one room without windows, category three were slightly better having two to four rooms and windows, category two were good farm houses or urban houses having five to nine rooms, class one consisted of all houses better than classes two to four.

Table 5.9 Number and categories of houses in 1841 and 1851

Category	1841	Percentage	1851	Percentage
First Class	235	5	264	5
Second Class	936	19	1,099	24
Third Class	2,408	48	2,526	55
Fourth Class	1,414	28	722	16
Total class one to four	4,993		4,611	
Uninhabited	258		398	
Total houses	5,251		5,009	

   In the period of ten years the total number of houses fell by 242 or by 5 per cent while the number of uninhabited houses rose by 140. There were modest increases in first, second and third class houses but class four houses were reduced by half. Many living in hovels either abandoned them or were evicted and their homes were demolished, while the more comfortable members of society were in a position to improve their accommodation. The existence of 258 uninhabited houses in 1841 would seem to indicate that clearance or abandonment of small holdings had started and continued during the decade.

A comparison of the housing statistics above with the position in the rural districts of Leinster shows a similar breakdown between the categories both in 1841 and 1851.

Table 5.10 Number and categories of houses in rural districts of Leinster

Category	1841	Percentage	1851	Percentage
First-class	6,714	3	8,426	4
Second-class	53,995	21	60,372	30
Third-class	119,404	47	105,581	52
Fourth-class	72,100	29	28,063	14
Total class one to four	252,213		202,442	
Uninhabited	8,030		11,926	
Total houses	260,243		214,368	

The similarity between the proportion of third and fourth class houses in Balrothery and the rural districts of Leinster shows that Balrothery, in spite of its proximity to the capital, was essentially a rural agricultural area subject to the vicissitudes and hardships of the agricultural economy.

The landlords managed to retain their estates and preserve their financial status for at least another generation. An examination of the records of the Landed Estates Court disclosed only two sales of land within the area in 1851 and nothing further until 1856. The large landowners, however, had their fears and difficulties during this period as expressed in a letter from George Hamilton that appeared in the *Dublin Evening Post* on 5 January 1847:

> The resident Irish gentry are placed now in a situation, perhaps, unparalleled in the history of any country. Surrounded by distress and suffering of the most appalling character, which it is quite beyond their power, and, I fear beyond even the power of Government, now to remove, reduced in their circumstances, in imminent danger of a social revolution in their own country, and of a confiscation of their own properties by some ill-considered measure of the British Parliament, this much calumniated body, disregarding all future considerations, are now remaining at their posts, devoting themselves to their local duties, and proving themselves the friends of the people.

Conclusion

This examination of the surviving material has shown that poverty and hunger existed in north Co. Dublin, although to a more limited extent than in many parts of Ireland. At the height of the distress in May 1849 the number in receipt of relief in the workhouse was 654, with 141 in the hospitals and 900 dependent on outdoor relief. In all 6 per cent of the population were then dependent on the poor law system, which was a smaller proportion than in most parts of Ireland, apart from the north. Even within the union destitution was not uniformly spread. Rates in the districts of Balbriggan, Holmpatrick, Lusk and Swords as shown in Table 4.3 were higher than in the remainder of the union indicating that a greater degree of destitution existed in these districts. These areas also fed the greatest numbers in the local centres during the period April to August 1847 as is evident in Table 5.1.

The aim of the 1838 act was to provide more effectual relief for the destitute poor. It would be pointless to attempt to speculate what would have resulted if the recommendations of the Commission of Inquiry presided over by Archbishop Whately had been implemented. The tragedy of that commission was that the work, so carefully carried out, was to become just a very valuable source for historical and social research rather than what they had hoped − the basis for new social policies in the 1830s.[1] Instead of seeking to provide employment the English poor law system was imposed without any adaptation to Irish circumstances. R.B. McDowell says:[2]

> The attitude of the commissioners clearly reflects their conception of their functions. They were not merely departmental officials engaged in guaranteeing the indigent Irishman from starvation, but warriors in a great administrative crusade. The poor law system, they were convinced, was bound to play a mighty part in inaugurating a new era in public life, when the prevalence of official impartiality, efficiency, economy and standardised and scientific methods of administration would raise the moral tone of the whole community.

This concept of an administrative crusade to reform the indigent Irish explains the constant parsimonious attitude of the commissioners to the most routine activities of the guardians, such as providing a meat dinner on Easter Sunday or some extra food to washerwomen, the cost of which would have come from the pockets of the guardians and those of other ratepayers. The commissioners, however, provided the genesis of a system of local government that served the country into the following century.

The guardians appear to have discharged their responsibilities well, while having regard to the constraints imposed on them by the Poor Law Commissioners. When the workhouse was full they quickly opened other relief centres. The number of relieving officers appointed was well in excess of the number recommended by the commissioners. They did not flinch from increasing rates in 1847 by amounts varying from 40 per cent to 300 per cent.

Some landlords, as well as being involved as guardians, played a leading role in providing relief outside the poor law system. In January 1843 a meeting of landholders and inhabitants of Swords was held for the purpose of providing employment.[3] The landholders present engaged nearly 50 labourers. Those who could not employ extra hands agreed to contribute to a fund to employ men in cleaning the town and providing footpaths. Their actions of course were not entirely altruistic. It was noted in the minutes of the meeting 'we deem it both our duty and our interest to do so'. It should also be noted that it took the advent of the poor law to make the wealthier members of society conscious of the need to provide employment for the poor by supporting Irish industry, as is evident from the report of the meeting in Balbriggan in November 1840. During the famine years a number of landlords made contributions to the district surveyor to enable him to employ men. Landlords were members of all relief committees. In March 1849 a circular was issued by Charles Cobbe, Junior, on behalf of the Swords Reproductive Relief Employment Committee to the landlords and ratepayers of the Swords Electoral District.[4] The circular gave particulars of work carried out in the previous two months that had been financed by a voluntary rate and from which 46 heads of families had benefited. Frances Power Cobbe of Newbridge in Donabate says in her book that 'numbers of ladies and gentlemen lost their lives by attending their poor' when stricken by fever.[5] Unfortunately she gives no more detail. Her father, Charles Cobbe, writing in his diary on 1 November 1845 showed his attitude to his tenants at the onset of the potato failure when he wrote: 'God open my heart and the hearts of others and may we show that we are Christians indeed and have imbibed the spirit of our master'.[6] Possibly due to his charitable concern and that of the other resident landlord in the area the district of Donabate showed the least decline in population between 1841 and 1851 having reduced by only ten persons. Should the landlords have done more? It is not possible to establish whether rents were reduced during the difficulties as any surviving estate papers are in private hands and not open to scrutiny.

The union was fortunate that after some unhappy experiences with staff in the early years two competent people filled the key roles of master and clerk during the height of the famine. Apart from the matron who died of fever shortly after opening, possibly because of negligence on the part of other staff, no other staff deaths are recorded in spite of the fact that many of the deaths in the workhouse were from contagious diseases.[7] Because of the sparsity of records it is difficult to evaluate the performance of the work-house. The mere fact that so little information is available would appear to show that after the early years, when it attracted criticism from the commis-sioners in their annual reports, the union got on with the business for which it was established without coming to general public notice. The workhouse provided a measure of fuel, clothing and diet to the poor as predicted in 1838 by the parish priest of Rush but to call the regime endured by inmates 'the salvation of the poor' could only be described as hyperbole.

George Hamilton, although he made strenuous efforts throughout the famine years to assist the poor of his area, saw the need to reform the system of potato dependency. Speaking in the House of Commons on 15 March 1847 he said:[8]

> If Ireland is ever to be raised from her present prostrate position, it must be by the Irish cottier being converted into a labourer, paid in money wages, learning to be industrious in his own country and no longer dependent on the potato, but upon his own labour and the sweat of his brow for subsistence.

The move in this direction which would have been inevitable was given an impetus by the events of the latter half of the decade.

Notes

DEP	*Dublin Evening Post.*	**RLFC** Relief Commission Papers.
PLC	Poor Law Commissioners.	**FCCA** Fingal County Council Archives.
RCB	Representative Church Body Library.	**NA** National Archives, Ireland.

INTRODUCTION

1 J. O'Connor, *The workhouses of Ireland* (Dublin, 1995), p. 47.
2 G. Nicholls, *A history of the Irish poor law* (London, 1856), p. 192.
3 *Return of every poor law union in Ireland, stating the population, area, number of landholders, and extent of landholdings*, HC 1845 (593) xxxviii.
4 *Freeman's Journal*, 25 Nov. 1840.
5 *Second report of the commissioners appointed to consider and recommend a general system of railways for Ireland*, appendix B, p. 14, HC 1837–8 (145) xxxv.
6 J. D'Alton, *The history of County Dublin* (Dublin, 1838), p. 232.
7 K. Whelan, 'The modern landscape from plantation to present' in F.H.A. Aalen, K. Whelan, M. Stout (eds), *Atlas of the Irish rural landscape* (Cork, 1997), pp 73–5.
8 Ibid.
9 M. Beames, *Peasants and power* (Sussex, 1983), p. 18.
10 A. Kettle, *Material for victory* (Dublin, 1958), p. 6.

CHAPTER 1

1 *First report from his majesty's commissioners for enquiring into the condition of the poorer classis in Ireland*, p. viii, HC 1835 (369), xxxii, hereafter referred to as *Poor inquiry*.
2 *Poor inquiry*, appendix D, p. 15, HC 1836 (36) xxxi, 1.
3 *Poor inquiry*, supplement to appendix A, pp 55–60, HC 1835 (369) xxxii, 1..
4 RCB, Vestry book, Swords parish 1834.
5 RCB, Vestry book, parishes of Clonmethan, Ballyboghal, Westpalstown, Palmerstown, 1837.
6 *Poor inquiry*, supplement to appendix D, p. 55, HC 1836 (36) xxxi, 1.
7 Cholera papers, Co. Dublin, NA, 2 440 8.
8 *Poor inquiry*, appendix D, p. 15.
9 Ibid., p. 16.
10 Ibid.   11 Ibid., p. 85.
12 *Poor inquiry*, appendix F, pp 43, 88, HC 1836 (38) xxxiii, 1.
13 Ibid., p. 88.

14 *Return of every poor law union in Ireland...* pp 394–5, HC 1846 (694) xi.
15 F.P. Cobbe, *Life of Frances Power Cobbe* (London, 1894), p. 188.
16 *Poor inquiry*, appendix E, p. 9, HC 1836 (37) xxxii, 1.
17 *Poor inquiry*, appendix D, p. 16.
18 *Poor inquiry*, appendix E, p. 9.
19 Ibid.
20 Ibid., pp 42–4.
21 Ibid., p. 43.
22 *Poor inquiry*, appendix D, p. 97.
23 Ibid.
24 *Poor inquiry, third report*, p. 3, HC 1836 (43) xxx, 1.
25 Ibid., p. 5.
26 Ibid., p. 34.
27 G. Nicholls, *poor laws – Ireland, first report to His Majesty's principal secretary of state for the home department* (London, 1838), p. 3.
28 V. Crossman, *Local government in nineteenth century Ireland* (Belfast, 1994), p. 45.

CHAPTER 2

1 *Fifth annual report of poor law commissioners*, pp 23–31, HC 1839 (239) xx.
2 Ibid.   3 Ibid.
4 *Freeman's Journal*, 20 Dec. 1838, *DEP*, 19 Dec. 1838.
5 *DEP*, 12 Mar. 1839.
6 NA, Orders, PLC, Vol 2, no. 64.
7 *DEP*, 2 May 1839.
8 *Sixth annual report of poor law commissioners*, p. 318, HC 1840 (253) xvii.
9 Nicholls, *Poor laws – Ireland, first report*, p. 41.
10 *Tenth annual report of poor law commissioners*, p. 182, HC 1844 (543) x.
11 As note 9, p. 30.
12 NA, Orders, PLC, Vol. 2, no. 65.
13 FCCA, Minutes, 28 May 1839.
14 Ibid.
15 *Sixth annual report of poor law commissioners*, p. 307.
16 *Dublin almanac 1839*, pp 201–2.
17 *Return of the number of magistrates ... in the different poor law unions in Ireland*, HC 1843 (347) xlvi.
18 *DEP*, 12 Mar. 1840.
19 *Reports relative to the valuations for poor rates and to the registered elective franchise in Ireland*, p. iv, HC 1841 (292) xxi.

20 FCCA, Minutes, 9 Nov. 1840.
21 *Eighth annual report of poor law commissioners*, p. 389, HC 1842 (399) xix.
22 *Minutes of evidence before the select committee of the House of Lords on the laws relating to the relief of the destitute poor in Ireland*, p. 840, HC 1846 (694) xi.
23 *DEP*, 25 June 1839.
24 Ibid.
25 G. O'Brien, 'The establishment of poor law unions in Ireland, 1838–43', in *Irish Historical Studies*, 43, (1982–3), p. 116.   26 Ibid.
27 NA, Orders, PLC, vol. 2, no. 71.
28 Ibid.
29 *Sixth annual report of poor law commissioners*, p. 307.
30 FCCA, Minutes, 18 Nov. 1839.
31 *Seventh annual report of poor law commissioners*, HC 1841 (327) xi.
32 *Reports relative to valuations for poor rates and the registered elective franchise in Ireland*, p. 3, HC 1841 (327) xi.
33 As note 31, p. 232.
34 *Freeman's Journal*, 25 Nov. 1840.
35 *Sixth annual report of poor law commissioners*, p. 135.
36 NA, Orders, PLC, vol. 2, no. 75.
37 *Report of commission for inquiring into the execution of the contracts for certain union workhouses in Ireland*, p. 102, HC 1844 (562) xxx.
38 Ibid., p. 23.   39 Ibid.
40 *Report of commissioner appointed to inquire into the execution of the contracts for certain union workhouses in Ireland, with a copy of treasury minute thereon*, p. 8, HC 1845 (170) xxvi.
41 Ibid.

CHAPTER 3

1 *Returns relating to poor relief, Ireland*, p. 51, HC 1843 (275) xlvi.
2 *Sixth annual report of poor law commissioners*, p. 39.
3 Ibid., pp 133–9.
4 Cobbe, *Life of Frances Power Cobbe*, p. 150.
5 H. Burke, *The people and the poor law in nineteenth century Ireland* (Dublin, 1987), p. 49.
6 *Tenth annual report of poor law commissioners*, pp 194–203.
7 Ibid.

8 *Sixth annual report of poor law commissioners*, p. 134.
9 *Seventh annual report of poor law commissioners*, p. 45.
10 *Eighth annual report of poor law commissioners*, p. 156.
11 *Seventh annual report of poor law commissioners*, p. 47.
12 Ibid.
13 *Appendix to eleventh report of commissioners of national education in Ireland*, p. 60, HC 1845 (650) xxvi.
14 *Appendix to fourteenth report of commissioners of national education in Ireland*, p. 107, HC 1847/8 (981) xxix.
15 *Appendix to eighteenth report of commissioners of national education in Ireland*, pp 184–5, HC 1852–53 (1583) xlii.
16 *Return of the number of children sent out to service from the union workhouses in Ireland in the years 1842, 1843, 1844, etc.*, HC 1845 (351) xxxviii.
17 Ibid.
18 *Eighth annual report of poor law commissioners*, p. 192.
19 Monument in Lusk parish church grounds.
20 *Eleventh annual report of poor law commissioners*, p. 150, HC 1845 (660) xxvii.

CHAPTER 4

1 *Eighth annual report of poor law commissioners*, p. 187.
2 Ibid.
3 *Hansard's parliamentary debates*, third series, lxv, col. 510.
4 NA, Minutes, 18 Nov. 1844.
5 *Minutes of evidence before the select committee of the House of Lords on the laws relating to the relief of the destitute poor in Ireland*, pp 837–47.
6 Letter dated 16 Nov. 1843 in *Report of commissioner appointed to inquire into the execution of the contracts for certain union workhouses in Ireland*, p. 102.
7 *Tenth annual report of poor law commissioners*, pp 336–59.
8 *Returns relating to poor relief Ireland*, p. 78, HC 1843 (275) xlvi.
9 NA, Orders, PLC, vol. 34, no. 109.
10 Ibid., vol. 36, no. 402/47.
11 NA, Minutes, 15 May 1850, BG40 A10.
12 Crossman, *Local government*, p. 47.
13 *Return showing the name of each union in Ireland, [etc.]* HC 1846 (262) xxxvi.
14 Ibid.
15 FCCA, Minutes, 17 Jan. 1842.
16 **1842 to 1845**: *Return of rates made in each union from the passing of the Irish poor relief act to the 5 Aug. 1845*, p. 539, HC 1846 (694) xi. **1846**: NA, St. Mary's Accession, Minutes, 10 Dec. 1845. **1847**: *Return of the valuation of each electoral district in Ireland and the total

poundage directed to be raised by any rate made during the year 1847*, HC 1847–8 (311) lvii. **1848**: Ibid. *Directed to be raised by any rate made during the year 1848*, HC 1849 (198) xlix. **1849**: Ibid. *Directed to be raised by any rate made during the year 1849*, HC 1850 (254) li. **1850**: Ibid. *Of rates levied during the year 1850*, HC 1851 (382) l. **1851**: Ibid. *Of rates levied during the year 1851*, HC 1852 (323) xlvii.
17 *Hansard 3*, ciii, col.1313.

CHAPTER 5

1 NA, RLFC1/10.
2 *Thirteenth annual report of poor law commissioners*, p. 122, HC 1847 (873) xxviii.
3 NA, Parochial Constabulary Returns, RLFC 4/9/01–55.
4 *Thirteenth annual report of poor law commissioners*, p. 183.
5 E.M. Crawford, 'Indian meal and pellagra in nineteenth century Ireland' in J.M. Goldstrom and L.A. Clarkson (eds), *Irish population, economy and society*, (Oxford, 1981), p. 118.
6 *Appendix to fourteenth report of select committee on poor laws (Ireland)*, pp 252–3, HC 1849 (572) xv, 11.
7 *Hansard 3*, lxxxix, col.195.
8 Ibid., col. 700.
9 *Papers relating to proceedings for the relief of distress and state of unions and workhouses in Ireland, eighth series*, p. 154, HC 1849 (1042) xlviii.
10 *Famine Ireland*, vol. 1, second series, pp 25–63 (IUP, Shannon, 1968).
11 *Thirteenth annual report of poor law commissioners*, p. 185.
12 NA, Orders, PLC, vol.36, no. 426/47.
13 *Evening Packet and Correspondent*, 8 Oct. 1846.
14 Ibid., 15 Oct. 1846.
15 NA, RLFC 3/2/9/23.
16 Letter dated 12 Feb. 1847 from George Woods to George Hamilton, NA, RLFC 3/2/9/2.
17 Letter dated 22 Feb. 1847 from George Woods to George Hamilton, NA, RLFC 3/2/9/3.
18 R. Keane, et al. (eds), *Ardgillan Castle and the Taylor family* (Dublin, 1995), pp 20–2.
19 NA, RLFC, 2/441/37, 10166.
20 Report 15 Apr. 1847 from R.H. Firth, District Surveyor, to the Grand Jury of Co. Dublin, FCCA, GJ 5/12.
21 Ibid.
22 *Supplementary appendix to the seventh and last report of the relief commissioners*, p. 29, HC 1847/8 (956) xxix.
23 Ibid.
24 S.H. Cousens, 'The regional variation in mortality rates during the great Irish famine' in *Proceedings of the Royal

Irish Academy*, 63, C, no. 3, p. 135.
25 NA, Orders, PLC, vol. 36, no. 255A/
26 *First annual report of commissioners for administering the laws for relief of the poor in Ireland*, p. 59, HC 1847/8 (963) xxxiii.
27 Ibid., p. 63.
28 Ibid., p. 64, HC 1847/8 (963) xxxiii.
29 Letter from W. Stanley, secretary to poor law commissioners, to Mullingar Poor Law Union in DEP, 18 Jan. 18
30 Irish Poor Relief Extension act, 10 Vic., s.10.
31 C. Kinealy, *This great calamity, the Irish famine 1845–52* (Dublin, 1994), p. 228.
32 Cousens, 'The regional variation in mortality rates', p. 142.
33 NA, Abstract of orders, PLC, vol. 3, 42/49.
34 *Return of number of persons under eight years of age in the workhouses of Ireland the third day of May 1849*, HC 1849 (609) xlvii.
35 *Census 1851*, V, table of deaths.
36 Ibid.
37 *Abstract of return of all medical establishments under the poor law in Ireland, union workhouses inclusive*, HC 1850 (758) li.
38 *Census 1851*, V, table of deaths.
39 *Third annual report of commissioners for administering the laws for the relief of the poor in Ireland*, p. 133, HC 1850 (1243) xxvii.
40 Ibid.
41 *Return of every poor law union in Ireland...* pp 394–5, HC 1846 (694) x
42 *Census 1851*, 11, agricultural returns.
43 Kettle, *Material for victory*, p. 6.
44 *Abstract of accounts showing the total amount levied under the authority of the grand juries in Ireland for each year 1843–1849*, HC 1850 (630) li.

CONCLUSION

1 Burke, *The people and the poor law in nineteenth century Ireland*, p. 36.
2 R.B. McDowell, 'Ireland on the eve the famine' in R.D. Edwards and T.D. Williams (eds), *The great famine* (Dublin, 1994 ed.), p. 52.
3 Minute of meeting of landholders and inhabitants of Swords and its vicinity, on 6 Jan. 1843, in private ownership.
4 Circular dated 24 Mar. 1849 from the Swords Reproductive Employment Committee to the landlords and ratepayers of the Swords Electoral District, in private ownership.
5 Cobbe, *Life of Frances Power Cobbe*, p. 182.
6 P. Bates, *Donabate and Portrane: a history* (Loughshinney, 2001), p. 147.
7 *Census 1851*, V, table of deaths.
8 *Hansard 3*, xc, col. 161.